Special Issue No. 2

THE LONDON & NORTH EASTERN RAILWAY

Edited by Michael Blakemore

Atlantic Publishers
Trevithick House, West End, Penryn,
Cornwall TR10 8HE

ISBN: 1 902827 04 X

© ATLANTIC PUBLISHERS 2001

Printed by:
THE AMADEUS PRESS LTD., BRADFORD

FRONT COVER
*LNER V2 2-6-2 NO. 4785 climbs out of
King's Cross past Belle Isle with an afternoon
express probably to Leeds and Bradford.
No. 4785 became BR No. 60814 in
June 1948 and features in an article by the
artist on page 30 of this book.*
Painting by A.B. Collins,
based on a photograph by the late E.R. Wethersett

CONTENTS

Fortunately No.3442 The Great Marquess *was saved for preservation and was purchased by Viscount Garnock on its withdrawal in December 1961. It was restored to LNER livery and during the 1960s it became one of the elite pioneers of preserved main line steam. On 6th March 1965 it was waiting outside Wakefield Kirkgate station to take over the 'Whitby Moors Rail Tour' for a farewell run over the Scarborough–Whitby and Whitby–Malton lines. In 1997 it made a nostalgic return to the West Highland line to run between Fort William and Mallaig.*
(Alan Tyson collection)

BELOW: *During 1959 the K4s were transferred to Thornton shed for use on freight traffic. No.61993* Loch Long *was photographed there in July that year.*
(C.J.B. Sanderson/Colour-Rail SC792)

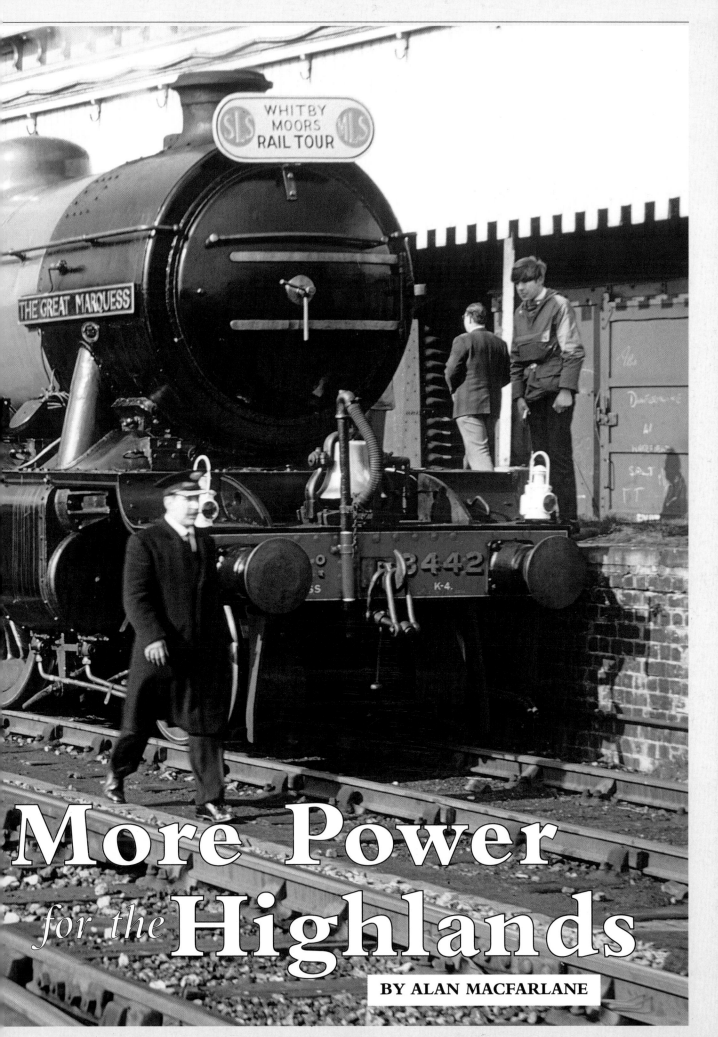

More Power
for the Highlands

BY ALAN MACFARLANE

LEFT: *A K4 on home territory – No.61995* Cameron of Lochiel *at Crianlarich on 18th June 1960 whilst working a special for the Stephenson Locomotive Society which brought it back to the West Highland line from exile at Thornton.*
(Derek Penney)

CENTRE: *A busy scene at Fort William depot on 18th June 1960 with* Cameron of Lochiel *on the vacuum-operated turntable and B1 4-6-0 No.61307 amongst the yard's other occupants.*
(Derek Penney)

LOWER: *Although Thornton regarded the K4s as freight engines, passenger work did still come their way from time to time. No.61996* Lord of the Isles *was photographed on a local at Thornton Junction in May 1959.*
(G.H. Hunt/Colour-Rail SC917)

The London & North Eastern Railway had a problem in the far North West of its territory on the former North British Railway's West Highland line. In the mid-1930s the line was too busy! The loadings on the line were too high for one locomotive and double-heading on a very high proportion of the passenger services was taking place. Light engine movements from Fort William back to Glasgow and double-heading of low-weight trains were starting to cause problems to the company. To reduce this practice a new locomotive capable of handling the now normal loads was requested.

The locomotives on the line at the time were 2-6-0 K2s and 4-4-0 'Glens'. The K2s had 23,000lbs tractive effort and were limited to an unassisted load of 220 tons; the 'Glens' on the other hand had only 20,260lbs tractive effort so they were limited to 180 tons. The 'Glens' had one more problem; as one driver said, 'they could slip in the Sahara'. The West Highland is not the driest place in the world!

With this as a background it was early in April 1936 that the LNER Chief Mechanical Engineer Mr. H.N. Gresley, no less, replied to Glasgow's management with a specification for the new K4. The designation of all 2-6-0 locomotives in the LNER was K. The locomotive was to be a three-cylinder 2-6-0 which met the axle loading requirement of 20

tons, the wheel spacing required by the civil engineers and the overall wheelbase short enough to suit the tight curvature of the West Highland line and the extension to Mallaig. At the time Doncaster was building 21 K3s which had been authorised on 21st January 1935 and it was suggested that one of them was built to the new three-cylinder Mogul design, the K4.

The Civil Engineers insisted on a bridge load test and working instructions were issued to the effect that no double-heading was to take place with any K4. On 21st April, after a test on the line's bridges had been carried out with the K4's designed load, the Chief Mechanical Engineer was informed that if the locomotive was within the Scottish Loading Gauge, he was to go ahead and build a K4. Gresley's ability to build for a specific use is well known and the K4 was to be one more.

Due to long delivery times on material, it was not until 24th February 1937 that K4 No. 3441 Loch Long was named in a ceremony at King's Cross. The next day *Loch Long* departed Doncaster for the north and her home shed of Eastfield, Glasgow. After running-in tests on the West Highland line it entered traffic on 3rd March, working goods trains from Glasgow to Fort William. Over the next two weeks, as the crew got used to the new loco-motive, the loading was slowly increased to 260 tons on 17th March and finally 300 tons. After the first few runs when the axle boxes 'ran warm', the temperature of all motion parts

settled down with no action being necessary.

Nigel Gresley confirmed on 5th April, a little over a year after the first plans were made, that the maximum load should be kept at 300 tons. In July 1937 the locomotive went into Cowlairs for minor modifications suggested by the crews and locomotive superintendent. The major change was the raising of the boiler pressure from its initial 180psi to 200psi. This by calculation raised the tractive effort from 32,900lbs to 36,900lbs, an increase of 11%.

The West Highland line is not renowned for high speeds but the K4s could and did show their speed and their capacity to accelerate through the outskirts of Glasgow. It is recorded that in October 1937 *Loch Long* with a 305 tons load, notched up to 22%, was storming along from Dumbarton to Craigendoran at 57mph. Other feats on the same journey were a speed of 28mph with the valve gear set to 27% all the way up to Gotland crossing, some six miles of 1 in 60 - 1 in 100. *Loch Long* was worked 'Gresley Style' with full regulator wherever possible, the cut-off being adjusted to maintain the required speed. She was fitted

with steam chest pressure gauge which differed from the boiler pressure by only 5lb psi. This difference shows how well designed the steam passages were.

The figures of speed, power and tractive effort can be given in several ways - as high a tractive effort as an A4, more power than a 'King' are only relative. The K4 was designed to climb mile on mile on gradients up to 1 in 60 with a maximum load. The boiler was not designed to give out this maximum output for a prolonged period but it was designed to recover from the high demand quickly. The boiler did come up to all expectations. The locomotive not only did the designed work which was 40% to 50% more than the loco-motives it replaced but, going from contem-porary reports, did so on the same, or less, water and coal.

As the trials were successful, it was decided to build a class of K4s. The request for a class was strong. The building budget for 1937/8 had been agreed so instead of waiting till the next year, and

The story of the
K4 No. 3441 LOCH LONG

No.1996 Lord of the Isles *approaches the County March (the Argyllshire/Perthshire boundary) north of Tyndrum with an up goods on 14th June 1948*
(B.V. Franey/J.L. Stevenson collection)

incurring the costs of double-heading, a change to this building programme was made. The changes noted were that six of the new J39s would not be built; in their place would be six of the new K4s. Each of the K4s was to cost £6,145 which was £1,420 more expensive than the already-authorised J39s at £4,725. This meant a total extra outlay of £8,500 for the class. Later that year, when one of the Scottish managers was on holiday, the order was reduced to five. Six J39s would cost £28,350. Five K4s were to cost £30,725 making an overspend of only £2,375. The J39s were again a Gresley design for a job, this time the Fife coal traffic. I wonder if the Scottish managers had to bargain 'East for West'.

The class of six was complete and in traffic by the end of 1938. All were allocated to Eastfield, with only Nos. 3443 and 3444 going the 107 miles to Fort William, the other end of the line, in October 1939. Five of the class remained on the line till 1959 before all were moved to Thornton and then for scrapping. The sixth, No. 3445 *MacCailin Mor*, departed to Doncaster in 1945 to be rebuilt as the prototype K1.

The introduction of this class reduced double heading by between 60 and 85%. This reduction in cost must have delighted the board as there is a lot of communications in the records on the excessive costs incurred with double-heading. Some of this correspondence, before the K4s arrived, is just on the point of "Please Explain", but that's another story!

The K4s were to the West Highland Line what the A4s were to the East Coast Main Line, both synonymous with the LNER and their designer, Gresley. Both types were designed for a job, both became masters of their work and both had three cylinders with 2-to-1 valve gear!

This is what Callum MacRaild (Driver, Fort William) has to say on K4s. "The K4s were run down by the time I was working them. They were grand engines for the banks but the Glasgow men ran them fast on the level sections to Craigendoran Junction and this took its toll on the locos. A powerful loco, a K4 will take ten up Beasdale".

Fortunately a K4 still exists. *The Great Marquess* is on the Severn Valley, at present waiting for its ten-year overhaul.

The names of the K4s and a short history of their working locations

3441 *Loch Long.*
In traffic 28-1-37 Eastfield, 24-4-59 to Thornton. Condemned 2-10-61, cut up Townhill (Dunfermline).
Nameplate centred on smokebox.
To No. 1993 14-9-46, to No. 61993 11-5-48.

3442 *MacCailein Mòr*-Incorrect spelling see note 1.
The Great Marquess 7/1938.
In traffic 6-7-38 Eastfield, 4-12-59 to Thornton. Condemned 18-12-61, sold to Viscount Garnock.
Original nameplate just fitted smokebox. After name change the plate overhung the smokebox. Font edge on front edge of smokebox.
To No. 1994 22-9-46, to No. 61994 15-10-48.

3443 *Cameron of Locheil.*
In traffic 20-12-38 Eastfield, 3-10-39 to Fort William, 25-5-54 to Eastfield, 9-12-59 to

No.61995 **Cameron of Lochiel** *passes Mallaig Junction, Fort William, c1949. The locomotive is still in LNER livery but has gained its new BR number.*
(T.J. Edgington collection)

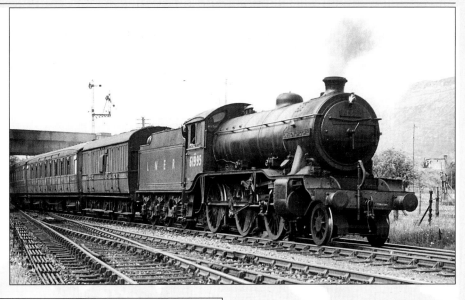

RIGHT: Cameron of Lochiel *again, departing from Fort William with a Mallaig train and passing Mallaig Junction c1949.*
(T.J. Edgington collection)

CENTRE: *No.3446* MacLeod of MacLeod, *in plain wartime black livery with the abbreviated 'NE' on the tender, passes Saughton Junction with a westbound goods on 27th February 1946.*
(J.L. Stevenson)

LOWER: *No.3442 as* MacCailein Mór.
(J.L. Stevenson collection)

Thornton. Condemned 2-10-61. Cut up Townhill (Dunfermline).
Nameplate overhung rear of smokebox.
To No. 1995 8-9-46, to No. 61995 3-7-48.

3444 *Lord of the Isles*.
In traffic 21-12-38 Eastfield, 23-10-39 to Fort William, 24-5-54 to Eastfield, 24-4-59 to Thornton. Condemned 2-10-61. Cut up

at Inverurie.
Nameplate just fitted the smokebox.
To No. 1996. 1-12-46 to No. 61996 27-11-48.

3445 *MacCailin Mòr*-Correct spelling!
In traffic 30-12-38 Eastfield till rebuilt as K1 at Doncaster 18-8-45.
Nameplate fitted smokebox. It was never renumbered or moved from Eastfield.

3446 *Lord of Dunvegan* – See Note 2.
MacLeod of MacLeod 3/1939.
In traffic 30-12-38 Eastfield, to Thornton 9-12-59. Condemned 2-10-61.
Cut up Inverurie.
Nameplate overhung rear of smokebox.
To No. 1998 4-5-46, to No. 61998 20-4-48.

Note 1
3442: name was fitted but the spelling was wrong as there are only thirteen letters in the Gaelic language. This also meant that the meaning changed. The correct spelling went on to No. 3445 from new. A photograph exists of No. 3442 with incorrect nameplate.

Note 2
3446: The Lord of Dunvegan was thought to be the Clan MacLeod chief. At the time this was a woman and it was thought this was the correct title - it wasn't.

LEFT: *A works photograph of No.3441*
Loch Long in photographic grey at
Darlington in 1937.
(The North British Railway Study Group Collection)

CENTRE: *With its later LNER number,*
No.1995 Cameron of Lochiel *stands outside*
Eastfield shed, Glasgow on 11th June 1948.
(J.L. Stevenson)

LOWER: *No.61996* Lord of the Isles *in*
the LNER/BR transitional period at Eastfield
on 14th May 1949.
(A. Noble)

A bit of Clan history and history of Fort William

To appeciate the story of No. 3442's nameplate you have to know something of Lochaber's (Fort William's) history. The new engine *Loch Long* was serviced at a shed within sight of Inverlochy Castle – and it was there in 1645 that James Graham, Marquess of Montrose, (the one they called The Great Marquess) soundly defeated a Campbell army under its chief, the Duke of Argyle. Montrose had been away in Campbell country killing Campbells and looting their property and while he was so engaged word came to him that the Duke of Argyle had been invested in Inverlochy Castle...Montrose hurried back to Lochaber, swooped on the castle and put 2,000 Campbells to the sword.

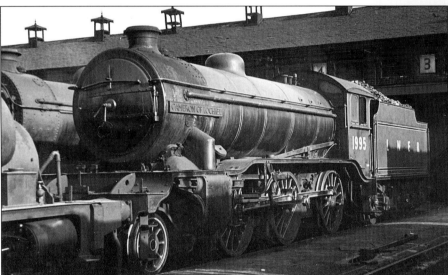

When No.3442 arrived at Fort William the local folk were puzzled to find that the engine bore the name MacCailein Mor. 'Mac' is Gaelic for 'son of', 'Mór' is 'great'. Cailin (the spelling is that of Innes of Learney, Lord Lyon King at Arms) was the founder and chief of the Clan Campbell. The new engine might well have been named Duke of Argyle. Why on earth had the LNER chosen to honour a man who had been no friend of Lochaber? The tale that went round Fort William was that the railway company had intended all along to honour the Marquess of Montrose but that some Sassenach (and the word can mean a Lowland Scot as well as an Englishman) had told them that MacCailein Mor was Gaelic for the Great Marquess. Anyway, the plate as it stood was wrong, there was a vowel too many in Cailein and the accent was missing over the vowel in Mór. No. 3442 disappeared into the shops and duly

LNER K4 2-6-0 Class 6, Superheated, mixed traffic, tender locomotive
Mileages and costs taken from mileage books and loco record cards

Number new	3441	3442	3443	3444	3445	3446
Number 1946	1993	1994	1995	1996	1997	1998
Date New	Jan 1937	July 1938	Dec 1938	Dec 1938	Dec 1938	Dec 1938
Cost New	£5,650	£6,433	£6,433	£6,433	£6,433	£6,434
Total Mileage in 1937	35,694					
1938	44,778	23,637	271	822	69	62
1940	33,009	38,565	55,506	53.557	50,162	45,086
1950	24,554	23,523	24,149	23,065	37,253	27,780
1960	16,835	16,618	10,385	18,527	0	13,680
Life mileage	628,153	672,088	575,478	607,323	606,158	632,527
Date condemned	2-10-61	18-12-61	2-10-61	2-10-61	12-6-61	2-10-61
Residual value	£1603-12-0	£1603-12-0	£1603-12-0	£1603-12-0	£1618-3-0	£1603-12-0

No.3446 MacLeod of MacLeod *near Glen*
Finnart in January 1940.
(C. Lawson Kerr/J.L. Stevenson collection)

emerged safely named in English The Great Marquess. The vanquished of Inverlochy had become the victor, the villain the hero. No. 3445 of the class was named *MacCailin Mór* and the erstwhile rival clan chiefs joined forces to improve the services on the West Highland line.

There were those who were not reconciled to a Campbell being commemorated in Lochaber. Clan history apart, had it not been a Campbell who had done his utmost to keep the railway out of his part of the Highlands? But Cameron of Lochiel was a happy choice for No. 3443, for a Cameron of Lochiel had put his weight behind every railway scheme in the history of Lochaber. No. 3444 was named *Lord of the Isles* and No. 3446 took the title *MacLeod of MacLeod*. It is perhaps a pity that the name-pickers did not go the whole hog and call it *Sir Rory Mór, MacLeod of MacLeod*. That would have been an engine name to remember and one big lump of brass.

Biography
Taken from papers kept in the Scottish Records Office. Ref BR/LNER/8-335. Information from the book *The West Highland Railway* by John Thomas.
The Glasgow Herald 2nd October 1937.
'LNER building Programme', LNER Study Group.
The LNER 2-6-0 Classes: Clay & Cliffe.

Loco in as-built condition as indicated by the boiler pressure of 180 psi. Increased to 200 psi during trials in 1937.

Now in BR lined black livery, No.61995 **Cameron of Lochiel** *makes a stirring departure from Fort William during the early 1950s.*
(T.J. Edgington collection)

RAVEN, COLLETT, GRESLEY & ELECTRIFICATION

BY GEOFFREY HUGHES

Early advocates of railway electrification found little encouragement from the mechanical engineers of the day – or, for that matter, from the managers. (The forced resignation of Col. O'Brien by the LMS in 1925, for over-persistent presentation of the benefits of electrification as he saw them, was the worst example)[1]. However, with less drastic personal results, other protagonists were equally unsuccessful. At the beginning of the century, when the technology was in its infancy, tentative proposals for partial electrification of Great Eastern and Great Northern suburban lines met such determined opposition that steam locomotives were specially built to demonstrate there was no merit in capital being invested in such schemes. That these locomotives were shown to be unsuccessful was quietly forgotten; Holden's 'Decapod' was a mechanical nonsense, while Ivatt's 0-8-2Ts were too heavy for the Widened Lines and found their true vocation in the coalfields of Nottingham and the West Riding. But the case for steam remained unshaken and the respective boards were no doubt hugely relieved to find themselves spared the need to take such pioneering decisions; the subject was not revived until the grouping. Both the GE and GN proposals were for third rail 650V dc supply, so at least the later cost of conversion to a higher standard was avoided.

However, in other parts of the country, limited suburban schemes did get commissioned – on the Lancashire & Yorkshire Railway and the North Eastern Railway north Tyneside lines at third rail 600V dc, as well as on the Brighton line with overhead ac. In fact, the early years of the century saw a considerable debate in professional circles on the merits of electrification, notably in the Institutions of Civil and Electrical Engineers, whilst the eminent consulting engineers Merz and McLellan presented a paper on the north Tyneside electrification to the 1904 meeting of the British Association. Charles Merz had developed the scheme and George Gibb, the then NER General Manager, persuaded his Board of the need to electrify, in the face of loss of traffic to the newly-introduced tramways[2]. Indeed, this should have been an example to be followed, as within three years business had recovered to the pre-tramcar level. But following Gibb's move to the London Underground in 1906, even the NER lost interest for the time being until, in 1913, after Vincent Raven had become CME, electrification of the 18½-mile mineral line between Shildon and Newport, intended as a trial for more ambitious schemes, was put in hand at 1,500V dc overhead.

In December 1915, at the height of the Great War, an interesting statement was made by H.M. Hobart in the course of the James Forrest lecture at the Civil Engineers, claiming "We are on the eve of the extensive employment of electric locomotives.... and the direct current system is the most appropriate". The speaker went on to regret the Brighton's decision to use a "German ac system, in view of the demonstrated success of dc locomotives"[3]. In 1920 the Ministry of Transport pronounced on the recommended form of electricity supply by specifying 1,500V dc as the future standard system, but did not indicate any preference between overhead or third rail. (This was to be superseded in 1956 by a general recommendation that new electrification should be at 25kV 50hz ac).

The North East of England was a leader in engineering innovation generally, in which extended electrification was an essential component, Merz and McLellan providing the expertise and NESCO, the main electrical supplier, anxious to develop its system. So, the post-war NER board also took the matter seriously and in 1919 considered a report submitted by Merz for the first main line electrification in Britain between York and Newcastle[4]. However, doubts arose about financial viability and, with the grouping on the horizon, the scheme did not go forward.

Sir Vincent Raven, back from his wartime job as Chief Superintendent of the Woolwich Arsenal, was now convinced that the future prosperity of the railways depended on electrification and became the country's leading advocate of this form of modernisation. To what extent he was friendly with O'Brien is not known, but the two did not engage in any joint work. Nor, unlike O'Brien, did Raven's advocacy of electrification lead him into conflict with his superiors. (It would not have affected the possibility of his becoming CME of the LNER at the grouping, as he was too old anyway). In fact, he received an appointment for a year as Technical Adviser to the LNER board, in which position he was nominally Nigel Gresley's superior. He was also chairman of the LNER Technical Committee, but this had limited interests, mainly to consider electrification proposals, and

No.6000 during its trials in Holland, hauling a train at Naarden-Bussum station in September 1947.

(Gresley Society collection)

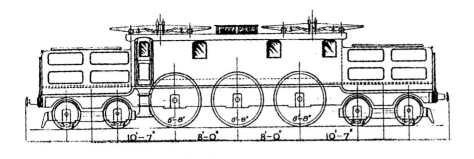

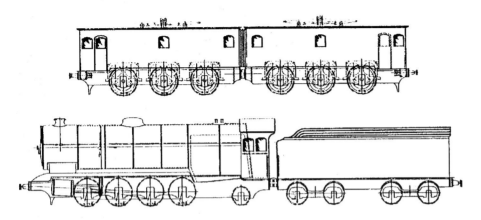

LEFT: *NER 4-6-4 electric locomotive No.13*

BELOW: *Raven's suggested 0-6-6-0 electric locomotive and the 0-8-2 steam locomotive with which he compared it.*

does not appear to have been used to discuss steam considerations. This was just as well, as Gresley and Raven were wide apart in many aspects of steam practice and Gresley would not have tolerated any interference with his plans. (It is of interest that on occasion three CMEs, past, present and future, attended meetings of the Technical Committee, as C.E. Fairburn, later of the LMS, represented the manufacturers English Electric). Raven also became a director of Metropolitan Vickers, as no doubt they hoped his connections would be useful in furthering their business.

Raven put his ideas into a major Paper presented to the North East Coast Institution of Engineers and Shipbuilders, read first in Newcastle in December 1921.[5] He proceeded methodically to compare the relative merits of steam and electric traction, dealing first with preparation time. "The steam raiser has to prepare the fire three hours before the footplate crew come on duty, after which a further hour is needed to complete the preparation of the locomotive. On the other hand, the electric locomotive, once cleaned and lubricated, is ready for immediate use, and can work continuously for twenty hours or more". Here, Raven seems to have gone slightly adrift, as he asserted that cleaning and lubrication could be seen to by the crew at wayside stops during running and between trips. This seems hardly practicable given the need for the footplatemen to keep vigilant when on the move, and to allow for rest periods between workings.

Turning to performance on the road, Raven contrasted the variable characteristics of steam with the predictable ones of the electric locomotive, saying that with electric operation average speed could be considerably improved without increasing maximum speed, so benefiting line occupation and traffic working. If double heading were necessary, two locomotives could be handled

by one crew. Moreover, coaling plant, watering facilities, ashpits and turntables would be saved by electricity, as would trains of locomotive coal, whilst regenerative braking could be used to save energy. A further advantage would be the increased comfort for the crews provided by enclosed cabs. He did not offer detailed cost comparisons, contenting himself by saying that he had gone into the matter carefully, taking into account all expenses concerned with the generation, transmission and distribution of electricity, together with capital charges and depreciation.

Sir Vincent thought that electrification would come by degrees and would depend on the availability of cheap power, adding that he saw no reason why waste heat should not be used in generation. He believed that because of their better overall load factor, the power supply companies should be able to generate electricity more cheaply than a railway company. Finally, he dealt at some length with the question of the design of electric locomotives, particularly the matter of mechanical power transmission, illustrating No.13, the locomotive which had been constructed as a prototype for the York to Newcastle electrification. Using 1,500V dc overhead supply, it relied on what is known as the 'quill' type of drive, employing an axle in a hollow shaft, connected to the wheels by helical springs, which was claimed to give greater flexibility than the conventional geared drive.

To illustrate the potential possessed by electricity, he went on to compare electric and steam locomotives capable of exerting a tractive effort of 60,000lb, about twice that of heavy freight engines then in common use. An 0-6-6-0 electric locomotive could conveniently be accommodated within the load gauge and could be handled by one man only, but a corresponding steam locomotive (he quoted an 0-8-2 tender engine) would be substantially out of gauge and would require a team of firemen to feed its 76ft grate. Again,

no figures of cost were provided, apart from the assertion that electrification would save 60% in coal consumption, and the coal could be of lower quality, using this to demonstrate the feasibility of a giant electric locomotive of a power which no steam equivalent could match. (He showed a number of lantern slides, as visual aids. Have any survived, I wonder?). Some of his statements were disputed in discussion; for example, it was claimed that he had ignored the possibilities of the Garratt locomotive.

Variations of his Paper were delivered on other occasions, notably at the summer meeting of the Mechanicals in Paris in 1923, but probably the least-known occasion was on 4th January 1923, at a meeting of the Great Western Railway (London) Lecture and Debating Society.[6] Taking place only a few days after the grouping had come into effect, the timing of the address is interesting, as is the venue, Paddington, and especially the chairman of the occasion who was none other than Charles B. Collett. On this occasion, Raven was careful to stress that he was dealing in a general way with the advantages of electricity and that his remarks should not be taken as applying to any particular railway. In his contribution from the chair, Collett, clearly impressed by Raven's arguments, said that the way Sir Vincent had reeled off the advantages of electric traction made them feel that this was better than steam. He asked why we in this country could not harness the coal in South Wales and so produce electricity more cheaply than in Switzerland. Also, he said, he for one would be glad to be relieved of the responsibility for high-pressure steam boilers.

Two other senior GWR engineers took part in the discussion. The first of these was Roger T. Smith, the company's Electrical Engineer, who compared the South Wales mineral lines to the NER Shildon electrification and thought that sooner or later it would pay the GWR to electrify them. (Smith, in fact, was quite outspoken in his support of electrification and had taken part in the original discussion at Newcastle, as well as addressing his own paper to the IEE on the subject).[7] The GWR Chief Engineer, W. W. Grierson, emphasised the heavy cost involved in electrification, saying there would have to be very considerably increased takings for conversion to be justified. The only experience they had was in two small London suburban lines, the Hammersmith & City, and the Ealing & Shepherds Bush. So, looking ahead to possible Great Western requirements of the future, they would be glad to learn of the experience of others.

Another contributor to the discussion was Fred V. Russell, for many years a strong proponent of steam traction on the Great Eastern. He was involved with the 'Decapod' of 1902 which, despite its own lack of success, was instrumental in steering his company away from the Liverpool Street proposals of the period. Later, he was responsible for organising the 'Jazz' service, to demonstrate again that steam could perform the job satisfactorily.

One wonders what behind-the-scenes

activity took place in arranging the lecture at Paddington. Raven and Collett are not known to have been close friends, although Raven was then President of the Association of Railway Locomotive Engineers and Collett a newly-elected member. They may have fixed the occasion informally at the summer meeting of the Association of Railway Locomotive Engineers, held in Scarborough the previous August. Possibly Roger Smith had also encouraged Collett to arrange the occasion. And were Raven and Collett perhaps flying a kite, hoping to attract attention to the subject at the commencement of a new era in British railway organisation?

It may be that more interest in electrification was taken behind the scenes than is generally appreciated. O'Brien's contribution has already been mentioned. He and Nigel Gresley had been friends at Horwich around the turn of the century, sharing a social life with the Aspinall daughters, but while O'Brien became involved in the Lancashire & Yorkshire electrification schemes, limited though they were, Gresley's future for the next 30 years was almost entirely steam-related. Nevertheless, his stance towards electrification is interesting, in particular his remarks in his Presidential address to the Institution of Locomotive Engineers in 1927: "This is an Institution of Locomotive Engineers, not an Institution of Steam Locomotive Engineers; all kinds of locomotives, steam, oil and electric, are our concern"[8].

However, he did not take actively to the cause of electrification, although in 1923, in a discussion at the IEE on the electrification of the Midi railway in France, he remarked that it was important that an electrified railway should possess its own power stations, to be independent of the public supply. In this, he was at odds with Raven. Ten years later he quoted the LYR electrification as costing the same to run as it had at its inauguration, whilst corresponding steam services were costing much less, and maintained that electrification was further off than it was twenty years before except for suburban lines. This being the period when he was introducing his P2 and A4 classes, no doubt he did not wish to see his work undermined by ideas that his advanced steam designs might be soon be overtaken by more efficient but less imposing electric machines – which he was heard to describe as "wireless boxes on wheels". Nevertheless, in 1936 preparatory work was commenced on Britain's first main line overhead electrification, the former Great Central route between Manchester and Sheffield – a scheme which had actually been in mind for several years.

In 1924 the LNER appointed an all-line Electrical Engineer to serve on Gresley's staff. He was H.W.H. Richards, who had worked on the Brighton suburban electrification. There was, of course, plenty for him to do, apart from electrification of the system – power supplies generally and installations in stations, workshops and depots, as well in coaching stock. But nothing firm was on the cards. The LNER board, without any serious discussion of the subject, had quietly let the NER proposals drop. Lacking Raven's enthusiasm, there was insufficient support from the NER directors who had joined the LNER board. However, in early LNER days consideration was again given

LNER Class EM1 Bo-Bo electric locomotive No.6000 is loaded on to the train ferry at Harwich in September 1947 en route for Holland and trials on the Netherlands State Railway.

(Gresley Society collection)

to schemes for the electrification of sections of the suburban lines out of King's Cross and Liverpool Street, but once more these plans were shelved. In 1929, the Government appointed the Weir Committee, of which the LNER Chief General Manager Sir Ralph Wedgwood was a member, to look into the prospects for main line electrification, but the committee made no substantive recommendations. In 1933 a comprehensive study was presented by Richards to the Institution of Civil Engineers[9]. In this he made technical and cost comparisons between steam, electricity and oil and was clearly taken seriously, as both Gresley and Wedgwood were present and took part in the discussion. Strangely, for such a well-developed paper, it did not attract wide attention.

However, despite the arguments of the professionals, such ventures into new technology had to wait many years and, apart from the third rail extensions of the Southern Railway, very little new electrification was completed before the grouping. The LNER electrified the south Tyneside lines and began conversion of the Great Central main line across the Pennines, but the Shildon line reverted to steam. In fact, the LNER finished its era with fewer electrified route miles than when it started. In 1939, the Great Western initiated a study – also prepared by Merz and McLellan – into the feasibility of converting the lines west of Taunton, but the business forecast for this project did not show much promise.[10]

So, we have Sir Vincent Raven, alone of the CMEs of the steam age, appearing as a whole-hearted proponent of electrification, but somewhat surprisingly Collett and Gresley also expressed views on certain advantages of conversion, although perhaps with less conviction. Moreover, one of the last two locomotives for which Gresley was responsible was the pioneer No.6701 (later No.6000), for which Metrovick, as with No.13, provided the electrical equipment. (The other was *Bantam Cock,* totally Gresley; both were intended for similar mixed traffic duties). No.6701 was also completed before the

line for which it was designed was converted, but it had the benefit of extensive testing and, although with modifications, eventually entered service to fulfil its design expectations.

Fortunately, Collett's anxieties about his responsibilities for high pressure boilers were unfounded, but it is perhaps ironic that of the trunk lines out of London, only that of the erstwhile Great Western remains unelectrified. But surely Sir Nigel realised that so far as Britain was concerned, he was not only leading the way in advanced designs of steam locomotives but of electric locomotives as well?

References

1. O'Brien had given a major Paper to the IEE in 1920, without apparently offending the LYR Board (he was Assistant CME to George Hughes at the time). However, it was his later Paper of 1924 which seems to have offended his LMS chiefs. This was The Future of Main Line Electrification of British Railways, read at several centres around the country. See *Proceedings Institution of Electrical Engineers* 61 (1924), also R.M.Tufnell *Backtrack* February 1999.
2. See R.L.Vickers: 'The Electric Trains of Newcastle', *Backtrack* March 1999.
3. Quoted in *Proceedings Institution of Electrical Engineers* 1921 p.61.
4. See R.A.S.Hennessey: *The Electric Railway that Never Was*, Oriel Press Newcastle, 1970.
5. Transactions, North East Coast Institution of Engineers and Shipbuilders, 1922, p13.
6. Records of the Great Western Railway (London) Debating Society, 1923, p23, also reported in *The Railway Gazette* 2nd February 1923.
7. *Proceedings Institution of Electrical Engineers* Feb. 1919.
8. Journal Institution of Locomotive Engineers 1927.
9. *Proceedings Institution of Civil Engineers* 1933 part 2 p23.
10. See Martin Smith; 'What Might Have Been', *British Railways Illustrated*, May 1999.

Bramhope Tunnel

BY JOHN EDGINGTON

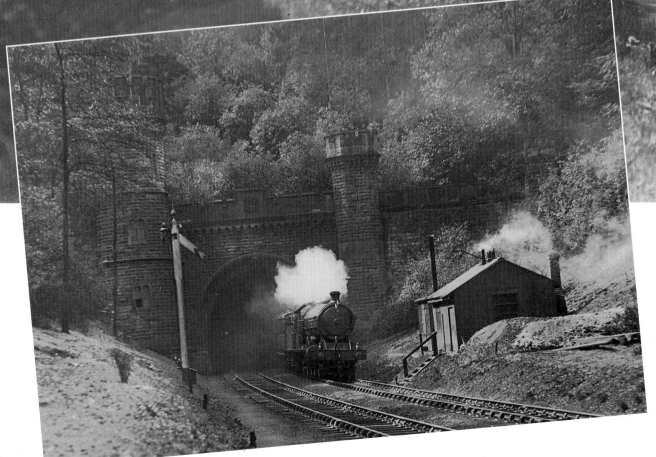

An up 'express' (note non-corridor coach) approaching the north portal of Bramhope Tunnel hauled by NER Class C7 4-4-2 No. 733 c.1927.

The North Eastern Railway was one of the four largest pre-grouping railways but, strange as it may seem, there were relatively few tunnels on the system. There was but one – and that only 98 yards long – on the East Coast Main Line between Shaftholme Junction and Berwick.

The longest NER tunnel by far was Bramhope, between Leeds and Harrogate, two miles 241 yards long. It was built by the Leeds & Thirsk Railway and authorised by its Act of Parliament of 21st July 1845. Construction lasted nearly four years and the final section of the Leeds & Thirsk including the tunnel was open for traffic on 9th July 1849.

The contractor was James Bray. Twenty working shafts were necessary, one with a maximum depth of 306 feet. Four of these were elliptical, 40ft x 30ft, and are the principal ventilating shafts. During construction 24 men were killed and there is a memorial to them in Otley churchyard.

Bramhope is an extremely wet tunnel and it was estimated that over 1,563 million gallons of water were pumped out during construction. Water has caused trouble ever since, including periods of closure or single line working to

LEFT: *A down express hauled by a NER Class B15 4-6-0 leaving the north portal. Arthington's distant signal is at clear indicating the train is for the Harrogate direction.*

Photographs by J.M. Tomlinson

The LNER tunnel cleaning machine at Arthington waiting a suitable opportunity to attack Bramhope Tunnel.

During one of the periods of single line working Sentinel railcar No. 2144 Traveller emerges from the north portal on a Leeds-Ilkley service running wrong road, probably about 1929. Traveller was new in December 1928 and it still looks pristine.

The memorial to the navvies in Otley church-yard photographed on 6th April 1991.

(T.J. Edgington)

Class A3 4-6-2 No. 2580 Shotover *approaches the north end of Bramhope Tunnel with the up 'Queen of Scots' Pullman.* Shotover *has the ACFI feed water heater fitted in July 1929. The bracket signals behind the rear coach are Arthington's home signals for Otley (left) and Harrogate (right).*

enable repairs to be carried out. The contractor's work may not have been of the best as at 9.30am on 19th September 1854 the up 'Parliamentary' from Stockton to Leeds ran into a pile of rubble. There were some injuries but fortunately no-one was killed.

The line is on a rising grade of 1 in 100 from mileposts 3 to 6 from Leeds, then after the summit through the tunnel and on to Arthington station the gradient falls at 1 in 94 for about three miles. In steam days freight trains were double-headed from Starbeck.

The line today, what is left of it, is a passenger-only route from Leeds to Harrogate and York but is probably busier than ever with a half-hourly interval service from Leeds to Knaresborough and alternate trains running through to York.

Jack Craig (1907-79) lived in Edinburgh until October 1926 when he made the journey west, to Glasgow, "to try and become an engineer" (he was successful!). Jack recalled that it was the 'sandwich' system - university between October and March and 'serving one's time' in the summer months. Despite a 47-hour week including till 12.30pm on Saturdays and much use being made of apprentices to work overtime and weekends, he was able to observe closely the railway scene, especially on former North British Railway lines, his first loyalty. From meticulously detailed diaries, he compiled the following account of the D49 4-4-0s' arrival in Scotland. The article originally appeared in the Gresley Observer (journal of the Gresley Society) No. 60 and is published again by very kind permission of Jack's widow, Mrs. Nora Craig.

THE D49 'SHIRES' IN SCOTLAND
BY JACK CRAIG

No.2756 Selkirkshire makes an impressive sight as it heads the 4.00pm Glasgow Queen Street to Leeds and Sheffield through Cowlairs station in 1929.

S ir Nigel Gresley is quoted as saying that the 'Shires' were not allocated to the Southern Scottish Area of the London & North Eastern Railway to take over the work of the ex-North British Railway Atlantics but there was a feeling among locomotive people that they were intended to take over from engines which were having increasing trouble with frames cracking. There were times when none of Haymarket's five Atlantics was in traffic

and the 'Scott' 4-4-0s were substituting with pilots for loads over nine coaches on the Dundee road. The NBR express engine stock at grouping on 1st January 1923 was 22 Atlantics and 43 'Scotts' (sixteen being unsuperheated) with 32 'Glens', though these splendid maids-of-all-work with 6ft driving wheels had their own particular preserves, notably the Glasgow - Fort William line. At grouping, the distribution (subsequent LNER

classification in brackets) was:-

Haymarket (HAY)	H (C11) 873/4/5/6/7; J (D29) 338/9/61; J (D30) 413/4/5/6/24/8; K (D34) 291.
St. Margaret's (STM)	H (C11) 510; I (C10) 901/3/4; J (D29) 895/7/9. 900; J (D30) 363, 400/17/23/6; K (D34) 266/78/87, 492, 502/3/4.
Eastfield (EFD)	J (D30) 410/1/97/8/9, 500/1; K (D34) 100/53, 221/41/2/56/8/81/98, 307, 405/6/7/8/90/3/4/5/6.
Dundee (DEE)	H (C11) 509, 868/9; I (C10) 902; J (D29) 243, 359/62, 896; J (D30) 419/20/1/2/5; K (D34) 505.
Aberdeen (ABD)	H (C11) 870/1/2; J (D29) 340.
Carlisle (Canal) (CAR)	H (C11) 878/9/80/1; I (C10) 905/6; J (D29) 360;
Hawick (HAW)	J (D30) 412/27.
Perth (PTH)	J (D29) 898.
Thornton Junction (THJ)	J (D29) 243/4; J (D30) 409/18; K (D34) 270.

At the same time, the number of main line trains to be worked was of the order:-

Haymarket	Four turns to Newcastle, three double turns to Dundee and one afternoon stopper, four double and four or five single turns to Glasgow ('Lothian Coast Express' in summer only).
St. Margaret's	Three turns to Carlisle, five to Perth and one to Dundee.
Eastfield	Five double turns to Edinburgh (two via Bathgate), a single and double turn to Fife.
Dundee and Aberdeen	Six return trains and a fish train between these cities, three Dundee - Edinburgh slows, one turn to Glasgow and the fish train on to Edinburgh.
Carlisle	Three turns to Edinburgh.
Perth	Two turns to Edinburgh, one double-headed for three back.

Thornton Junction, Dunfermline, Hawick, Bathgate and Berwick all worked their diagrams with 'Glens' and the 'Intermediates' (to become Classes D32 and D33) and representatives of Class M that were to become Class D31.

In winter months it appears that there were sufficient main line engines (Haymarket also had four ex-North Eastern Railway Z Atlantics - to become Class C7 - Nos. 714, 2193/4 and 2204, mostly for going south but venturing to Glasgow on the lighter trains). There were some extra trains on Saturdays and excursions for football fixtures and for the rugby internationals in Edinburgh, also heavy traffic during Edinburgh and Glasgow holidays when there was a borrowing of engines from opposite ends, mostly 'Glens'.

So, after grouping, in the second half of 1924, the engine strength was much boosted by the arrival of 24 new 'Directors' of Class D11/2. Their allocation was:-

Haymarket	6381/2/3/4/5, 6401.
St. Margaret's	6389/90/1/2/9.
Eastfield	6378/9/80/97/8, 6400.
Dundee	6386/93/4/5/6.
Perth	6387/8.

In late summer of the same year five Class A1 Pacifics, Nos. 2563 - 7, were allocated to Haymarket entrusted to Drivers Henderson, Davidson, Roper, Shedden and Smith with four Newcastle runs (and a rest week), the 7.35am Edinburgh - Glasgow (sleepers and steel diners in the formation) and c. 11.20am slow back (invariably piloted by Queen Street's shunter No. 9832 up Cowlairs rather than being 0-6-2T-banked). There was a movement of some 'Scotts', such that they took on less important trains, notably at the main sheds though Aberdeen gained three to help with piloting the increasingly heavy

trains to Dundee, en route to Edinburgh.

Thus, with the support of Atlantics, 'Scotts' and 'Glens', the number of express engines appeared to be ample and in winter some of the St. Margaret's 'Directors' were stored. But between mid-December 1927 and the end of August 1928, there arrived in Scotland fifteen Class D49 'Shire' 4-4-0s with eight more following between 20th February and 20th June 1929. Their allocation was as follows and no obvious intention to supplant the Atlantics is apparent:

SHED	ATLANTICS	'SHIRES'
HAY	9510 *The Lord Provost*	264 *Stirlingshire*
	9874 *Dunedin*	270 *Argyllshire*
	9875 *Midlothian*	
	9877 *Liddesdale*	
	9878 *Hazeldean*	
STM	9873 *Saint Mungo*	265 *Lanarkshire*
	9901 *St. Johnstoun*	277 *Berwickshire*
	9903 *Cock o' the North*	281 *Dumbartonshire*
	9904 *Holyrood*	306 *Roxburghshire*
		311 *Peebles-shire*
EFD		2753 *Cheshire*
		2754 *Rutlandshire*
		2755 *Berkshire*
		2756 *Selkirkshire*
		2757 *Dumfries-shire*
		2758 *Northumberland*
		2759 *Cumberland*
		2760 *Westmorland*
DEE	9509 *Duke of Rothesay*	246 *Morayshire*
	9868 *Aberdonian*	249 *Aberdeenshire*
	9869 *Bonnie Dundee*	266 *Forfarshire*
	9902 *Highland Chief*	307 *Kincardineshire*
		309 *Banffshire*
		310 *Kinross-shire*
ABD	9870 *Bon-Accord*	
	9871 *Thane of Fife*	
	9872 *Auld Reekie*	
PTH		250 *Perthshire*
		329 *Inverness-shire*
CAR	9876 *Waverley*	
	9879 *Abbotsford*	
	9880 *Tweeddale*	
	9881 *Borderer*	
	9905 *Buccleuch*	
	9906 *Teribus*	

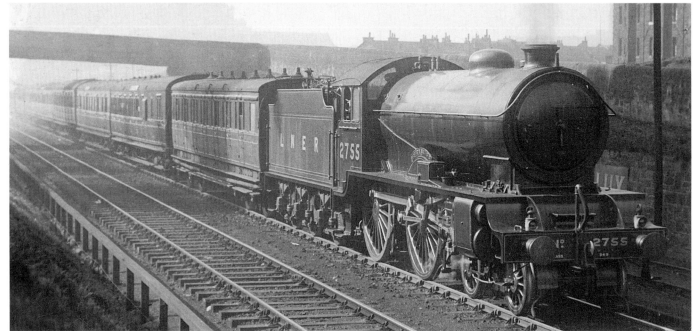

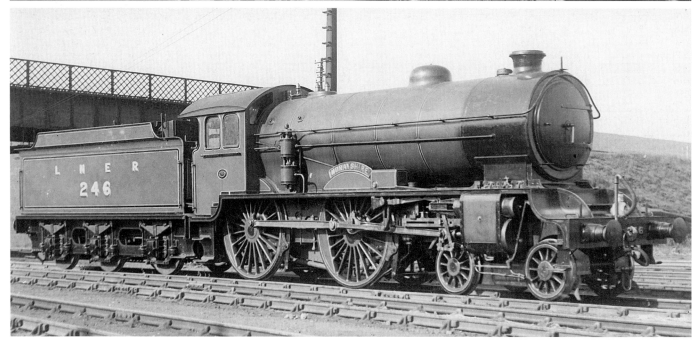

No. 329 *Inverness-shire* didn't settle down happily and went south to York within a couple of months of its initial arrival at Perth. It returned in the summer of 1929 but, nomad-like, it departed again for York at the beginning of autumn. It was February 1931 before it was re-allocated to Perth but within days the 4-4-0 was despatched to Eastfield where its sojourn was to last six-and-a-half years! Nos. 2754 *Rutlandshire* and 2758 *Northumberland* were at Eastfield briefly (approximately three months) before taking up residence at Haymarket and St. Margaret's respectively. Also two 'Shires' initially allocated to the North Eastern Area at York enjoyed spells north of the border:- No. 352 *Leicestershire* at Haymarket for the first three weeks in the spring of 1929 and No. 336 *Buckinghamshire* at Perth for a longer spell between November 1929 and February 1931.

At St. Margaret's, the 'Shires' largely took over from the 'Directors' on the 6.25am stopper to Dundee, returning with a similar service, the 4.21am fast to Perth and 8.30am express back, the 6.40am stopper and slow back, the 7.29am fast and the 12.25pm fast back, the 2.06pm fast and the 5.28pm slow back, the 4.31pm slow and heavy 8.10pm express back. An Atlantic was usual for the last turn, particularly as the return load was over 'Scott' - 'Director' and possibly 'Shire' load unpiloted, the 'Shire' being allowed one and an Atlantic two coaches more than a 'Scott' or 'Director'. The Atlantic (goatee-bearded Fettes was one of the drivers) may have 'doubled' with an earlier turn, 4.21am or 7.29am ex-Waverley, or the 'Shires' may have been on duty. The 4.21am had the King's Cross - Inverness sleeping carriages during the winter months (off the 'Aberdonian') whilst the 7.29am had a first class sleeper and through carriage for Perth off the 10.25pm 'Night Scotsman' ex - King's Cross. The 8.30am fast from Perth conveyed a composite for the 'Flying Scotsman', the engine being suitably headboarded. The late 8.10pm had the Inverness - King's Cross sleepers between October and May, hence the heavy load. During the summer months when the Inverness service ran independently from and to King's Cross, the through carriages came up from Perth at 9.10pm. An additional stopper from Edinburgh to Perth was also provided, leaving Waverley at 12.30pm, so that the balances became: 12.30pm return 5.28pm, 2.06pm return 8.10pm, 4.31pm return 9.10pm. The engine of the morning run to Dundee was available for a later turn like the 2.06pm to Perth.

It was some years later that St. Margaret's had one or more turns to Glasgow, notably the 8.25pm back with a Cowlairs stop for any fish traffic to be transferred from the 2.15pm ex-Mallaig. Of the three turns to Carlisle it was usual for two to be Atlantics and the third - with the light 12 noon (load six) returning with the equally-light 6.29pm, due Waverley at 9.06pm - to be D49-hauled. Both trains, incidentally, conveyed a restaurant car, also

No.2753 Cheshire *comes over the top of Cowlairs bank with the 4.00pm express from Glasgow Queen Street to Leeds City. The leading vehicle is for Sheffield Victoria, to be detached at York. This photograph was originally published in the October 1929 issue of the* LNER Magazine.

composite and third brake to/from St. Pancras. This working was entrusted to No. 311 *Peebles-shire* for a long time (no records exist of the 'Directors' being involved) and later No. 2758; it was *Northumberland* that took a curve near Carlisle too fast on the 12 o'clock and overturned itself and part of the train, sadly with three fatalities.

The Haymarket engines were utility and seldom replaced 'Directors' on the four double turns to Glasgow with Nos. 6381/2/3/5 and for which 6384 and 6401 were 'stand-bys'. There was a number of single turns at 9.05am out, 1.00pm back and later 11.10am out and the heavy 4 o'clock back, along with the Saturday 6.29pm collecting the two front coaches off the 'Flying Scotsman' (arrived 6.15pm at Waverley) and back on the 10.40pm. These were all possible jobs for Nos. 264 and 270 and later for No. 2754. Then there were three double turns to Dundee, most trains changing engines there and going on to Aberdeen with the 'Shires' (piloted as necessary, pilot working next the train) covering for the Atlantics as necessary. Turn No. 1 was 4.15am ex-Waverley ('Aberdonian') back by 9.40am with three coaches for the 'Flying Scotsman' and a composite brake for the 'Thames-Forth Express' (10.05am to Carlisle and St. Pancras), afternoon 2.12pm and back at 7.27pm. Turn No. 2 was 7.35am with coaches off the 'Night Scotsman' back at 1.23pm, then the afternoon 4.25pm (simultaneous departure from Waverley and Haymarket with the 4.25pm Glasgow slow!) and back by 9.22pm. Turn No. 3 was 9.30am to Dundee, back at 4.14pm (seldom over 'Scott' load), the 6.31pm

nine-coach train (eleven on Saturdays) with three coaches from the 'Flying Scotsman' and brake composite from St. Pancras on the 'Thames-Forth Express', then back at 10.50pm with 'Aberdonian' sleepers - about 240 miles for the day. Going south was less usual unless on an afternoon meat train, back piloting an evening arrival from Newcastle. Saturday extras to Glasgow (sometimes worked straight back 'empty') could have any engine including a 'Shire'.

For running-in purposes, where a big engine like a Pacific was concerned, two slows were 'paired' and a swap made in the turns, ie. instead of the 7.35am express from Edinburgh to Glasgow with the sleeper from London, the 5.50am slow was used, the balance being the 11.16am slow back. The 5.50am slow engine, the return working of Eastfield's Nos. 9410 or 9500 off the newspapers, was elevated to the 7.35am. And instead of the 4.00pm Edinburgh - Glasgow and 7.45pm slow back, Haymarket took the 2.46pm slow and Eastfield's engine off the 10.11am semi-fast took the 4 o'clock. For running-in Atlantics (and, I think, 'Shires') the three Larbert turns were used and the regular Nos. 9595/6/7 stood down. These were 3.27pm and 5.31pm ex-Waverley, one being seven coaches with three coming back, while the 4.00am returned a Haymarket engine going out light. Later, Polmont got 'Glen' No. 9408 for the job - less far to run light.

There were six trains either way, expresses, between Dundee and Aberdeen, all those northbound starting from Edinburgh and changing engines at Dundee. The Dundee and Aberdeen Atlantics were first choice and as trains got heavier so pilots were in regular use. Shortage of Atlantics meant that Dundee's six 'Shires' were impressed but more often they were concerned in three turns to Edinburgh and back, stoppers both ways, early, mid-morning and early afternoon. There was also the up fish from Aberdeen, due

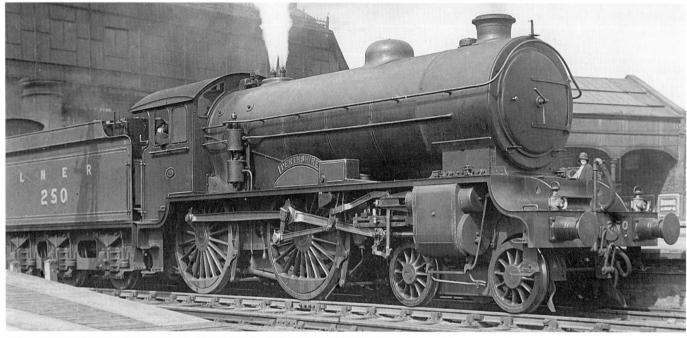

Cowlairs station in 1930 and No. 2757 Dumfries-shire *and K2 2-6-0 No. 4704 receive the signal to descend to Glasgow Queen Street to work the 4.55pm ex5.11pm slow to Edinburgh respectively.*

in Edinburgh around 5.00pm, having changed engines at Dundee and being Atlantic-worked throughout, possibly over Atlantic load on occasions. The engine worked out backwards to Corstorphine before reaching Haymarket to turn and return was the late evening 8.10pm semi-fast. That Atlantic could have been visiting Edinburgh for a second time, following an early slow from Dundee and ex-Edinburgh on the 10.15am Aberdeen express.

So to Perth, a shed noted for the immaculate condition of its engines. Two engines (from 'Scotts' Nos. 9243/4 and No. 9418, then 'Directors' Nos. 6387/8 and now 'Shires' Nos. 250 and 329) were required for Edinburgh trains. These were the 6.20am stopper and back on the 10.07am ex-Waverley with through carriages for Inverness (also Keith during the summer season), while the afternoon turn was the 3.22pm ex-Perth with two engines (one from the morning turn) and balancing coaches from the Highland section. If the connection was late (and that, happily, had become unusual), two trains ran, both with a Perth 'Shire' or 'Director'. One engine collected the Perth coach off the 'Flying Scotsman' departing Waverley at 6.37pm. The second engine ran to Corstorphine backwards and returned home on the last train of the day at 9.25pm. No. 329, as already recorded, didn't settle down well and during one of its longer spells south of the border between September 1929 and February 1931, York sent No. 336 *Buckinghamshire* as substitute in November 1929. No. 246 was transferred from Dundee in August 1930

A rather more intimate knowledge was gained of the Eastfield 'Shires'. It was interesting that while Haymarket's main turns were covered by four 'Directors', each double-shift-

ed, Eastfield had six 'Shires', each with own driver and each doing a single turn or about 95 miles a day. The engines and their drivers were: Nos. 2753 (Reidman), 2755 (Menzies), 2756 (Ramsay), 2757 (Thomson), 2759 (Carrie) and 2760 (Miller). There was no 'utility' locomotive to cover shoppings so a 'Director' was standby or more likely a second turn was worked by a 'Shire'. When the seventh roster was added, Driver Forbes from the Perth runs and No. 329 joined the team in February 1931. The jobs c.1930/1 (and with changes pending, notably the loss of the 4 o'clock) were:

1. 7.44am fast and back 10.40am stopper.
2. 8.55am fast and later to Leith Central where the engine turned to form the 12.45pm through to Glasgow (1 o'clock ex-Waverley) and piloted by a Class C16 4-4-2T between Central and Waverley.
3. 10.11am semi-fast and back 2.46pm stopper.
4. 4 o'clock fast (destination Leeds with through carriage to Sheffield Victoria, later 2.05pm), back 6.29pm with coaches off the 'Flying Scotsman'.
5. 4.55pm fast, back 8 o'clock stopper.
6. 5.11pm slow, back with the 'Queen of Scots Pullman' (7.42pm ex-Waverley).
7. 6.00pm fast (with through carriage for King's Cross), back 9 o'clock fast (with through carriage from Southampton).

There were many changes to follow, with different balances on Saturdays and with the withdrawal of the stopping trains. The 'Shires' were in demand in the period of

Sunday excursions, notably on the Montrose trains (maximum load of ten) though Nos. 2753/5 do not seem to have run so often.

A very unusual working of the Whitley Bay excursion (normally Eastfield-worked to Edinburgh and a long 'book-off') was a train from Queen Street's Platforms 1 and 2, assembled at the last minute and with the engines in the tunnel mouth. These were Haymarket's No. 270 and St. Margaret's No. 306, which must have been at Eastfield overnight and when it was thought that such a pairing was not allowed.

In very happy vein, footplate runs are recalled, both in darkness with Dobson (spare link) on No. 2759 on a Sunday return excursion from Dundee to Glasgow and when Thomson's fireman got me out of the late Sunday evening train (one of two 'Shire' turns) in Waverley to be on the footplate to Falkirk.

In the 1930s the 'Shires' might have come into their own as the Atlantics began to be withdrawn from May 1933 but Pacifics Nos. 2745/8/9 became Carlisle's mainstay and some of its Atlantics, for the remainder of their lives, were transferred to help at Haymarket, Dundee and Aberdeen.

By degrees, Haymarket in particular and later Dundee and even Eastfield (when through engine working to Newcastle was in mind) had large allocations of A1 and A4 Pacifics, V2 'Green Arrows' and the Mikados. All those took over the traffic, including slows, between Edinburgh, Dundee and Aberdeen, along with a lot of the Edinburgh - Glasgow and Edinburgh - Perth trains (where even St. Margaret's K3s were used), so all 4-4-0s in Scotland dropped back to the lesser trains.

NBR section schedules and loadings were not generally severe and the 'Shires' had a not too arduous life, though with a good deal of hill work. The 47 miles between Edinburgh and Glasgow remained a best timing for only certain trains of 60 minutes; the 2.12pm Edinburgh - Dundee, 59 miles, was allowed 80 minutes non-stop while the 4.21am Edinburgh - Perth, 48 miles, was allowed 68 minutes non-stop.

OPPOSITE PAGE:
TOP: *A rare treat for Whitley Bay excursionists in 1929 as Nos. 270* Argyllshire *and 306* Roxburghshire *disturb the Sunday morning peace on Cowlairs bank.*
CENTRE: *An appropriate location for No.250* Perthshire *at the head of an Edinburgh-bound express at Perth station in 1929.*
LOWER: *Cowlairs bank and a group of observers on the bridge watch No. 264* Stirlingshire *climbing past with an Edinburgh-bound train (probably the 10.11am semi-fast) in 1930.*

THE LNER –
A Character Study

BY JOHN VAN RIEMSDIJK

Photographs from the author's collection

The grouped railways did not have long to develop integrated personalities and had hardly grown up before the Second World War inhibited their individuality, yet characters they did have and, as with human beings, it was possible to trace these to heredity and environment.

The Great Western was all heredity; it hardly changed, but it was a special case. The Southern evolved to suit its environment and this meant electrification, but its constituents were evidently compatible so that the amalgamation under very good management was amicable and purposeful. The LMS was the result of an enforced marriage of rival sub-groups, both south and north of the Border, which was only workable because it was not poor and was fairly ruthlessly run as a firm on the American pattern. Its inheritance was unhappy and this showed until the challenge of nationalisation conjured up loyalties previously unsuspected.

The LNER was not without internal rivalries and conflicting loyalties, but it still seemed to cohere. Perhaps there was a realisation that its contituents had to pull together to survive and a sort of folk memory of, for instance, the antagonism which the Great Northern had had to face in its earlier years.

There was also justifiable pride in what the LNER had inherited and, later on, in what it achieved. In a way, it seemed a high-spirited railway and echoed the audacity and skill of Lord Faringdon, Sir Sam Fay, Lord Claud Hamilton and some others who had fought for its constituents. On the engineering side, the perfect embodiment of this character was Nigel Gresley.

These impressions are, of course, personal to someone who was born in the year after the LNER came into existence, who has known many older railwaymen at different levels of responsibility from directors downward and who has read a great deal of railway history, like so many of us. They are tinged with affection resulting from long and close familiarity, which started at birth.

As a very small child, I watched 0-6-2 tanks, clean, black and neatly lettered, pulling golden-coloured teak coaches with white roofs past the end of the garden. Yes, the coaches were clean and many of those articulated sets had white-rimmed wheels. This was surely the

A splendid parade at King's Cross shed on 13th September 1938 covering the span from Great Northern Railway single No. 1 to LNER streamlined A4 Pacific No. 4462 Great Snipe, with locomotives from the Stirling, Ivatt and Gresley eras.

most beautiful livery ever applied to railway carriages anywhere, splendid though the Pullman cars or the blue giants of the International Sleeping Car Co. appeared in my eyes. I also watched ancient 0-6-0 tender engines shunting coal wagons in the sylvan setting of Cranley Gardens. Those engines were also neat and clean, though their ability to slide along the track with wheels locked probably impressed me more.

The fact that the LNER was in no hurry to cast away its locomotive inheritance gave a certain paradoxical unity to the system because neat, black, long-funnelled locomotives, though of a multitude of types, were to be found everywhere. Of the carriages they pulled one can only say that there was great variety there also and while the exteriors were generally clean, the interiors were decidely dusty. It has been said that the LNER was run by country gentlemen and even its shabby corners were not without dignity.

The retention of so much from the past was not merely a matter of economy, it was also a

mark of respect. The locomotives were a very good lot, on the whole, and their retention on so large a scale undoubtedly helped to earn the loyalty of the older employees and soften the impact of more modern machines. Transfer of motive power occasionally was unsuccessful - 'Directors' and 'Faringdons' were not very well received at King's Cross, nor were Ivatt 4-4-0s at Haymarket - but there was little acrimony. In fact the LNER was a railway of good manners and one heard many stories about this, some from before the grouping. There is the story of the gentleman who went into Gresley's outer office when Gresley was Carriage & Wagon Superintendent and enquired if it might be possible to speak briefly with him. "I will go and see", said the newly-appointed clark, "Who shall I say wants to see him?" "Tell him it's Mr. Ivatt", came the reply. An echo of this, from many years later, came when H.N.G. was working in his office and not to be disturbed. Hearing a considerable rumpus in the outer office, he went to the door and called "Please come in straightaway,

Mr. Thom". R.A. Thom was a fine boiler engineer, but noted as a creator of disturbances in offices. Ivatt also provides one of the finest examples of tact in engineering design, by the way he introduced his Atlantics. Starting with No. 990, which the enginemen could easily recognise as an enlarged Stirling single, to be fired and driven in much the same way, he paved the way for an enthusiastic reception of his big-boilered version.

One could tell similar stories concerning Robinson and Raven and James Holden, but one has to admit that there seems to have been rather more pugnacity north of the border.

One's impressions of a character are often affected by superficially trivial things which may yet be very significant. The LNER inherited far more locomotives with roomy, side-windowed cabs than the others. On frequent visits to Holland with my parents and brother, I used to gaze admiringly upon the cabs of the 'Clauds' and, above all, on the cab of the engine attached to the Hook or

*A panorama from the new coaling plant at King's Cross 'Top Shed'
completed in 1931, with a line-up of well-cleaned motive power. Prominent
among them is A1 4-6-2 No. 4474 Victor Wild. Other representatives are
from Classes 01 2-8-0, C1 4-4-2 and K3 2-6-0, then come the three
Gresley Pacifics and lastly four J6 0-6-0s. A GNR J52 0-6-0ST
No. 4241, as shed pilot, is receiving attention.*

Flushing Continental boat train in which we
were to travel – a '1500' class in original condition. When these beautiful engines gave way
to 'Sandringhams' the luxury look did not
suffer much from the slight reduction of the
fireman's walk. Marylebone, too, sported
desirable residences behind the fireboxes, most
amply on the 4-6-2 tanks, while further north
side-window cabs were to be seen on almost
all the locomotives.

This was quite unlike what could be seen
in the earlier years of the other group railways
and the LNER standardised such cabs from
the beginning, while the other three groups
continued production of the more open type
right up to the war. Whether this care for the
footplate crew was symptomatic or not is a
matter of opinion, but the Great Northern
did not conform until the first Gresley Pacific
arrived. One remembers a Great Eastern driver

working into King's Cross on a train from
Cambridge with an Ivatt Atlantic; he waved
his hand around the cab and declared
"Mechanically this engine is first class, as good
as any of ours, but this is not place for a man
to spend his life".

Everybody knew that the LNER was
nearly insolvent, an inheritence from the Act
of Parliament which gave it birth, yet it had
the effrontery to do things with unmatched
style and so to provoke irritation (if not
worse) at Paddington and Euston. Ageing
Atlantics on Pullman trains running to very fast
schedules, as on that other northern railway
across the Channel, were taking passengers
from under the noses of their rivals, enormous
trains of varnished teak were making the

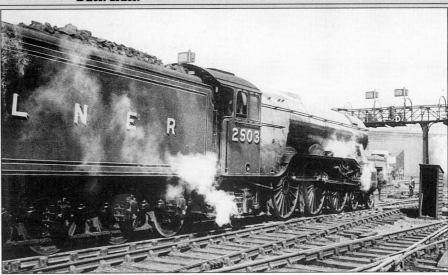

A3 4-6-2 No. 2503 Firdaussi *departs from King's Cross and heads towards Gasworks Tunnel. A superbly-evocative picture of a majestic locomotive design.*

acteristic which totally defies the camera is, of course, the sound.

The two sounds which were the sole property of the LNER were the 'Gresley Beat' and, less well-remembered, the ringing sound of the motion on the Pacifics and some others. This was due to the use of high-tensile alloy steels to reduce weight, which conferred elegance on the motion parts and a peal of bells when an express passed at speed. It was not noticeable in the train, but magnificent when heard at a wayside station. It disappeared when, in wartime, carbon steel replaced the alloy steels and it never came back. Resonant steel was also used for buffer heads for a time; one could make them ring by throwing a small stone at them. Later buffer heads produced no music.

As for the Gresley beat, the ignorant have widely misunderstood and disparaged it. It is a straightforward geometrical fact that a 2:1 gear with horizontal levers can give a better steam distribution than is possible when horizontal levers, even cranked as in GWR practice, are used to conjugate inside and outside valve movements in a four-cylinder engine. Also, irregularity in exhaust beats is more audible when six beats are involved than with only four and anyone who has listened to the finest of inside-cylinder 4-4-0s at speed knows that, because of short connecting rods, such engines often produced only one discernible exhaust beat per turn of the wheels, or perhaps a loud pair and a soft pair, unevenly spaced. The moment of release to exhaust is not the most sensitive point in valve events and timing a locomotive to regularise it is purely audible cosmetics. Gresley's disregard of this was perhaps another piece of LNER effrontery, but it was also highly intelligent engineering.

Lastly, let us remember that the LNER gave us the first proper railway museum, at a time when other group railways were scrapping admired relics, and it gave a home to locomotives from the Southern and the Great Western as well. As enthusiasts, historians and preservers, we must feel grateful for this example of the sense of history, of family, indeed of heredity. That it was provided by the LNER was entirely in character.

A3 No. 2580 Shotover *on the turntable in King's Cross loco yard. This view of its new corridor tender (received in April 1928) symbolises the innovative nature of the LNER and a human touch is added by the crew standing in the corridor connection.*

world's longest non-stop service runs and eventually the fastest train in Britain was no longer to be found on the Great Western. All this was a bold, brave effort to become more profitable and raised the morale of almost all the LNER staff. The war doomed the LNER but also proved how effective an organisation it had become, thanks to engineering excellence and a very real family spirit.

While the visual character of the LNER is amply documented by photographs, the mental character could not be photographed, but there are yet some views which are expressive in this way, by the grouping of the persons before the camera or perhaps the posing of a train in a particular location or on a particular occasion. But an essential and individual char-

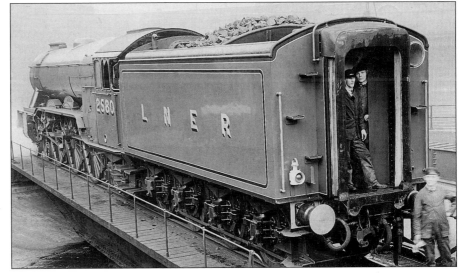

SOS

Bert Collins writes of his experiences with locomotives which were 'short of steam'

Photographs from the author's collection

If there was one consistency that characterised steam locomotives, it was their inconsistency. No matter how famous the class, or successful its designer, it was a near certainty that every class would produce not only its star performers but also the occasional rogue. Footplatemen were generally tolerant of bad riding, draughty and unpleasant working conditions and much else, but it was shortage of steam (SOS) that gave the most grief.

There was enough happening on the footplate without the men having to worry about the engine's inability to make steam. This article seeks to discuss - from a personal viewpoint gained from footplate experience - a few rogue engines amongst the works of Sir Nigel Gresley.

As a young enthusiast, I spent the war years from 1939 - 1945 in North London following the comings and goings of the East Coast Main Line of the LNER where, of course, Sir Nigel Gresley's engines prevailed. At that time, it was not necessary for me to carry notebooks. I had seen all the locomotives on view so many times that the visit of an unusual engine was committed to memory and could be checked when I returned home.

In August 1947 I joined the LNER at King's Cross Top Shed as a cleaner and I passed as a fireman in June 1948, spending the next decade on the footplate at both King's Cross Top Shed and Hornsey. Before I commenced my short railway career, I paid regular visits to King's Cross and, like many other enthusiasts, I watched proceedings from the end of Platform 10 (now Platform 8). The main attraction was always the A4s and to witness the end of a corridor tender as it appeared from the smoke haze of Gasworks Tunnel never failed to arouse emotions. We knew that it would be one of some thirteen corridor tender-fitted engines based in the Southern Area at that time.

During the war years most main line workings had been truncated and London engines and men seldom worked further than Grantham and return, which allowed the enginemen home between shifts rather than having to lodge away. Among the star attractions were No. 2509 *Silver Link*, No. 4498 *Sir Nigel Gresley* and No. 4489 *Dominion of Canada*. If the engine was No. 4489, we were not to know that the crew on board were in for a distinctly uncomfortable day's work. When we admired this once glamorous engine as it backed on to its train, clad in its wartime livery of filth, we were unaware that the engine had built up an unenviable reputation for poor steaming. By a quirk of good luck, when I transferred from King's Cross to Hornsey I found myself rostered in the local

goods link with Driver Bill Gilbey. Bill had been a fireman in the Top Link at King's Cross before World War II and, knowing that I was an enthusiast, he was happy to recount his exploits on the streamlined trains. Bill recalled that No. 4489 was never a popular engine. Although at that time she was not a bad steamer, she refused to boil water in the manner of her sisters. Whereas most A4s steamed freely, with No. 4489 every pound of steam had to be worked hard for. As a consequence, it was necessary to adjust the locomotive's management by nursing the engine along. It was a question of easing or shutting the regulator, where possible, to allow the injectors to top up boiler water levels when needed and to add a few extra pounds of steam on the clock. Very often time was lost with the hope of regaining the odd minute elsewhere and using recovery time if the working timetable allowed - not a satisfactory method of running prestige trains. No. 4489 was always being booked SOS.

Despite innumerable examinations at Doncaster Works and King's Cross, and several boiler changes, the problem was never solved. As a young cleaner at King's Cross, I was put to work as a footplate cleaner on main line engines. I remember working on No. 4489 (now renumbered No. 10) and watched as the engine crew arrived, looked at their mount and disappeared into the foreman's office. They were seen later on a rundown V2 - preferring a rough 'Green Arrow' that steamed rather than a smoother-riding A4 that did not! I understand that conversion of No. 10 from a single chimney to double blastpipe and Kylchap brought a marked improvement in No. 10's steaming behaviour.

Shortage of steam could be attributed to several reasons. Very often poor shed maintenance (such as blocked tubes, smokebox and ashpan) contributed, whilst poor-quality coal gave rise to poor steaming and inexperienced engine crews could also face trouble. All these difficulties could be

overcome, but sometimes with some classes a latent design fault was more serious.

K3 2-6-0s were certainly rogues for different reasons. These engines developed a justified reputation for rough riding. The silly piano stool seats with which they were fitted did not help. When the engine bucked there was a tendency to throw one back off the seat towards the tender making it necessary to hang on to the cab side. Quite often, and in particular on a rundown engine, the cab side sheets seemed to have a mind of their own as they oscillated in three-quarter time up, down and sideways as if they had no intention of forming part of the engine's permanent fabric.

It was possible to use a short tank engine shovel when firing a K3 and by regularly keeping the back end of the firegrate full, with an occasional shovelful down the sides, the engine would produce all the steam required.

The same could not be said of the N2 0-6-2 tanks. Although the N2s were a development of existing Ivatt and Gresley designs, as a class their steaming was erratic. The N2 boiler was based on an Ivatt design and used on subsequent Gresley classes. On the Ivatt 4-4-0s, 0-6-0s and N1s the boiler seldom gave trouble. It was ironic that the last type of locomotive to use this boiler from new should be so unreliable given the intensity of work that the class was called upon to perform. In all probability the N2s incorporated draughting faults that were never fully investigated or understood. After Gresley's death, it was decided to replace the

indifferent Doncaster 'Twin Tube' superheater with the proven 'Robinson' type. Although the Robinson superheater did much to ameliorate the N2's poor steaming, it was never completely successful. A number of LNER-built N2s were fitted with taller chimneys for engines destined for work outside the GN Metropolitan area. Presumably these chimneys were provided in an attempt to assist draughting although no official information on this has been forthcoming. Most of these long chimneys were removed after World War II.

At King's Cross, I was first rostered in the shed duty link with a young driver. One afternoon we were booked 'As Required' which necessitated reporting to the shed foreman for duties. We were given a list of train arrivals and told to relieve the crews at King's Cross station and bring the engines up to Top Shed for disposal. Amongst the arrivals was the 'Yorkshire Pullman' which had a mid-afternoon arrival time. A glance at the arrival board indicated that the train was several minutes late and would arrive at Platform 7 (now 6). We sat on a luggage trolley to await the arrival of the train. An almost spotless No. 60056 *Centenary* headed the train and as she gently drew the train to a stand her safety valves lifted. The sound of a Pacific's safety valves was extremely loud and in the confines of the train shed at King's Cross that noise was amplified. As the valves lifted they drew water from the over-filled boiler, spraying water over disgruntled passengers and also badly soiling their clothes.

We climbed on to the engine to find the crew in a filthy state and the footplate in total disarray. The driver, speaking with a selection of well-chosen expletives, instructed my mate to book the engine SOS and with that they left us to it. When we looked at the fire we were horrified to see a boxful and it was still extremely hot. My mate instructed me to keep the engine blowing off steam for a while until sufficient water had left the boiler and we could then attempt to keep the engine quiet by working the injector just as steam pressure reached the red mark. It was all in vain. The fire was so hot that she rapidly made steam and blew off again.

Word reached the station locomotive foreman who hurried to us to see what the trouble was. My mate explained, with language similar to that which the train driver had used, the dilemma which faced us. Meanwhile station staff were doing all they could to mollify the public. Whilst the engine was still blowing off steam we felt it prudent to duck below the cab side windows to avoid the possibility of outraged passengers giving vent to their anger and blaming us for a problem that was not of our making. The locomotive foreman ordered our immediate release from the train which was drawn off us and we were given green lights to Belle Isle and the sanctuary of Top Shed.

It transpired that the engine had given trouble on the entire run from Leeds and in their anxiety the crew had over-reacted by firing the engine too heavily and at Hitchin, or thereabouts, forgot that they had more than enough fire on to get them to King's Cross, but continued firing the engine as far as Hatfield or Potters Bar with disastrous results. When we arrived at Top Shed, two firedroppers were assigned to deal with the engine and I did not envy them their task. I never did discover whether the engine was at fault or whether the crew were not up to their job on that occasion.

After a few years at Hornsey shed, I was rostered into Hornsey's 'Main Line' link. 'Main Line' was something of a misnomer in that Hornsey men seldom found themselves working on the main line proper, with all the principal work going to King's Cross and their colleagues at provincial sheds further down the ECML.

Our work at Hornsey was the movement of mineral traffic between New England (Peterborough) and Ferme Park (Hornsey) and the return of empty wagons northwards. By its very nature this traffic was consigned to the slow and goods roads throughout its journey with main line running restricted to such places as the two-track bottlenecks at Greenwood and Digswell.

The Main Line link consisted of some 40 turns of duty of which six were rostered to be worked throughout between Ferme Park and New England and then, because the trip could

No. 60814 looks world-weary as it struggles with an up freight near Brookmans Park on 10th March 1956. It was just a few weeks before this photograph that the author experienced an uncomfortable trip on the footplate of this locomotive, as described in the text.

take up to six hours, we returned home as passengers on service trains. All remaining turns in the link were mostly to Hitchin and back, together with a few South London workings.

My regular driver felt that six turns to New England were insufficient to justify his signing of route knowledge north of Hitchin so that when Peterborough turns came round

I was booked with an alternative driver. A favourite turn was No. 1090 down, 6.05am on duty, 7.30am ex-Ferme Park. My driver on one occasion for a week on this turn was Bert Robinson. Bert was an ebullient, twinkly-eyed character who originated from the Great Eastern - Kings Lynn, I believe. He was also a very good engineman.

Our engine for the day was an anonymous New England 'Austerity' 2-8-0. These engines were never ones to inspire any great enthusiasm but, although they seldom received much in the way of attention at their parent depot, they clattered about with their work and they were irritatingly reliable. Our train was about 75 empty wagons and we left Ferme Park on time. The trip to Hitchin was uneventful and we duly arrived promptly at Hitchin South on the goods line where we were booked to take water. With the tender tank replenished, Hitchin South's home signal was raised and we trundled down to the station, where we were brought to a halt. Ominously, an engine crew were standing on the north end of the platform. We were to be taken off! This procedure did occur occasionally, much to our annoyance, since the odd trip to Peterborough on a day turn was something of a rarity.

We walked across to the crew's mess hut, situated on the up platform, and Bert went round to the foreman's office at Hitchin shed for orders. As we were eating our food a message came from the foreman's office informing us that a No. 1 fitted freight was coming up the platform road and we were to relieve the crew and take the train forward to King's Cross Goods Yard. The men were a lodging crew who were on overtime and the authorities were anxious to get them home as quickly as possible so that they could be ready for the following night's return working.

We made our way to the south end of the up platform to await the train's arrival. It was

As explained in the text, K3s were normally free-steaming engines. K3/6 No. 2448 stands at Hitchin at the head of a pre-war semi-fast. Some twenty years later the author would begin his adventure with No. 60814 from the same spot.

V2 2-6-2 No. 4785 strides towards Harringay with a down fitted express freight - probably the much-vaunted 'Scotch Goods'. It would become No. 60814 on 8th June 1948 - ironically the author's sixteenth birthday!

a 'Green Arrow' on about 45 wagons fully brake-fitted. I always enjoyed a trip on a V2 and this one looked immaculate in BR black lined livery that had been polished like a pair of guardsman's boots! As she approached, I could see that she was No. 60814 - a Top Shed engine! The driver drew the train to a halt alongside the platform water crane where water was taken. The driver and fireman whom we relieved remarked that the engine was a bit shy of steam.

Whilst the tank was filling, I put on a good fire. The coal seemed of a fair quality and was burning nicely. As an aid to good steaming, I always tried to keep the back corners full on a wide firebox. Once the tank was full, we were away straight out on to the main line. The boiler was fairly full of water and I reckoned that a few good shovelfuls around the grate would be more than adquate as we passed Wymondly and made our way towards Stevenage.

One of the most thrilling sounds of steam was that of a Gresley V2, slightly out of kilter at the front end, and in full flow performing the work for which it was intended - express brake-fitted freight. To be on the footplate of one under such conditions was an added bonus. But things were not quite right on No. 814.

We left Hitchin with a good head of steam and the boiler adequately filled. I knew the fire was right so why was she not making steam? As we approached Stevenage, it was essential that the exhaust injector was used. But since we left Hitchin steam had fallen back to about 190lb psi and as soon as the injector was worked she started to fall back in steam alarmingly, not that the engine seemed to mind as she dashed along nicely. What should have been an enjoyable ride was rapidly developing into a minor nightmare.

My priority was to ensure that water was constantly visible in the gauge glasses. Bert was sitting in his seat, seemingly unconcerned as he sang to himself. What confidence those old engine drivers had! He had been working the engine with full throttle, with the lever set at about 18% cut-off, but as we ran through Knebworth Bert eased the regulator allowing me the opportunity to get a little water into the

N2 0-6-2T No. 4768 was a long-time stablemate of the author's engine No. 69531 at Hornsey, eventually becoming No. 69547. It is pictured at Harringay Up Goods.

boiler. We were running with about 160-170lb psi and I did not wish the engine to go below that. Moreover, I did not want to fall into the *Centenary* trap of continually throwing coal on to the fire in the vain hope of improving the engine's steaming. I was conscious of the need to start the process of running the fire down, knowing that a heavy fire in the grate on arrival at King's Cross Goods Yard would create the problems that had beset the crew of *Centenary*.

I managed to juggle with the steam and water as we approached Welwyn Viaduct with about 175lb psi on the clock and half a glass of water showing in the boiler. I was determined to be in my seat as we raced through Welwyn Garden City and, as we expected, a King's Cross suburban link N2 driver spotted us and proceeded to greet us with a somewhat ungallant whistle code. Bert eased the regulator enabling me to get some more water in the boiler to help us on the final lug from Hatfield to Potters Bar. A few more rounds of coal and I hoped that that would be the end of stoking for the day. As we passed Potters Bar, I felt able, at last, to take it easy. At New Barnet the regulator was closed and on went the injector. The excitement was over - I thought. Although the trip, so far, had been no more than 20-odd miles, it had seemed like a hundred! I was beginning to feel that I had let my mate down. As we coasted down through suburban north London, King's Cross men were persistently greeting us with derisory signals on the whistle, knowing that a pair of Hornsey upstarts was in control of one of their thoroughbreds. I am not so sure that

they would have felt the same had they been working on this particular engine!

There was one more surprise waiting for us. When we entered Oakleigh Park Tunnel the down-draught created as the engine entered the tunnel caused a rather nasty blowback. In the anxiety that had gone before, I had forgotten the cardinal rule when coasting towards a tunnel at high speed - it was blower on and damper shut. Luckily for both of us, we were seated and no harm ensued. However, it did demonstrate to me that because we seldom ran fast trains, we lacked the expertise of more experienced express train crews. It made sense, therefore, when the management eventually decided to diagram a fully-fitted brake fish empties train to Hornsey men. This train consisted of two ex-south London fish empty trains coupled together. The train originally started out of Clarence Yard (Finsbury Park), but was re-routed to start from Ferme Park instead; we worked through to New England.

At Finsbury Park, we were turned in from the main line to the goods line and from there we were straight into King's Cross Goods yard. After all the shenanigans that had gone before, it was satisfying to look into the firebox and see a nice thin level fire covering the grate.

Our train was pulled off by a pilot engine and we were released into Top Shed. Once more King's Cross men were looking down their snouts at us; King's Cross and Hornsey men never did hit it off and Hornsey men were on one of their engines! Bert stopped the engine just short of the turntable and went to book her in. Meanwhile, an old Top Shed chum of mine, Sid Webb, happened along and saw me on the footplate. Sid had been a friend of mine from schooldays when we watched trains together as kids and our friendship continued when I joined the railway at Top Shed in 1947. When we met on No. 814 he had already graduated as a top link fireman. "Hallo Bert", he said "I see you've been on one of our best today. How did you get on with her?" I spewed out our sorry tale to which he replied "Well done. I had her up from Newcastle the other week and the most steam we had all the way was 150 and we lost

A3 No. 56 Centenary *(named after the 1925 Stockton & Darlington centenary) stands at Finsbury Park on an up express. After its next visit to Doncaster Works it would emerge as No. 60056 in BR blue livery, ready to give a young and inexperienced crew an embarrassing and unpleasant hour in King's Cross station!*

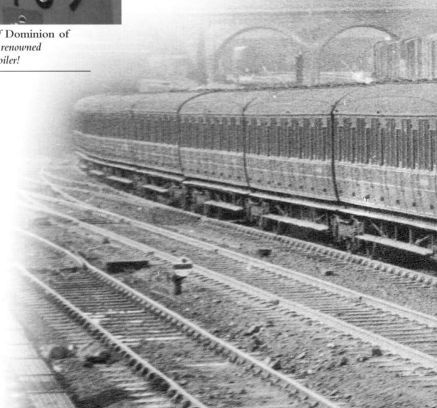

Sir Nigel Gresley peers quizzically from the footplate of Dominion of Canada. *Perhaps the crew have tried to explain - with renowned Cockney diplomacy - the shortcomings of the engine's boiler!*

Before compiling these notes, I happened to re-acquaint myself with O. S. Nock's *Locomotives of Sir Nigel Gresley* and on page 49 I noted a run with A1 No. 4476 *Royal Lancer* with Driver Taylor and Fireman Luty on board. This legendary pair will be remembered by some for their exploits on the inaugural run of the 'Silver Jubilee' in 1935 with A4 No. 2509 *Silver Link*. Although the boiler on No. 4476 was pressed to 180lb psi, it was interesting to note that there were times when the engine was running, seemingly quite happily, with as little as 160lb with a train of 500 tons. Whilst I would not be so presumptuous as to make comparisons, I wonder if Bert Robinson knew a thing or two?

Incidentally No. 60814, in the condition in which I worked on her, was used in the making of the feature film *The Ladykillers*. She was glimpsed shunting mineral wagons in and out of Copenhagen Tunnel. At that time many would think that that was all she was good for!

This article has not been written as a discussion on the 'pros' and 'cons' of locomotive design faults and the shortcomings of those who worked on them. These points have been written up many times elsewhere by learned and distinguished writers and engineers whose technical knowledge has given pleasure to many of us. My intention was to try and show that work on steam locomotives was not always the glamorous job that some enthusiasts believed. At times the work could be hard and trying and thousands put their trust in those up front, unaware of the drama that was unfolding and of the skills that they applied in tackling the problems I have tried to explain.

time all over the place". Bert returned to the engine and said he had reported her SOS. Apparently they knew all about her and said she was going to be stopped for examination. Later we learned that the reason for the lateness at Hitchin was that the crew we had relieved had been forced to stop at various locations along the line for shortage of steam and they had consequently lost their path.

We had a wash on the engine - the toilet facilities at Top Shed were notoriously disgusting - and made our way down to King's Cross station and home to Hornsey. On the way down Bert casually remarked that they were open! That is still the best pint of beer I have ever had!

A4 Pacific No. 60010 Dominion of Canada *leaving Haymarket shed, Edinburgh, to work south on the non-stop 'Flying Scotsman' c1948. The two crews were to enjoy a less than satisfactory trip on this engine due to its notoriously poor steaming. Note the carefully trimmed and stacked coal in the tender which allowed up to an extra ton over the nominal capacity.*

As a class the N2s were indifferent steamers but No. 69531 was a notable exception. The author was rostered with this locomotive on a regular basis for an enjoyable year, finding her both strong and nippy. It is seen climbing past Belle Isle c1959.

DONCASTER IN THE THIRTIES

BY A. F. COOK

This is one of the last articles written by the late Arthur Cook in response to a personal invitation to contribute to this LNER Special, just before his passing in 1999. He had hoped to obtain a pupillage at Doncaster, but the circumstances of the pre-war years prevented this. He writes here of his early acquaintance with the LNER, with the enthusiasm which was to remain with him through his life. After gaining his MA at Cambridge, he made his career in higher education in his chosen subject of mechanical engineering, eventually becoming Principal of Macclesfield College. Arthur Cook has written widely on technical aspects of LNER and LMS locomotives, but sadly did not complete a full-length book, which would have been an education to us all.

I had the great good fortune to be a schoolboy in Doncaster in the 1930s. Fortunately my fellow railway enthusiasts and I realised that we were living in what was then the most exciting railway centre in the country and we made the most of it. In this we were helped by a number of things: no major locomotive works had such good views from public roads as Doncaster Plant; much of the activity at Doncaster shed could be viewed without approaching the shed offices, and at Doncaster Grammar School Tuesday and Thursday afternoons were devoted to games, so that for those

who managed to dodge games, there was the possibility of getting to the railway in daylight on four days a week, even in mid-winter. In those days enthusiast visitors to sheds were rare and I got to know all the shed foremen, so that for some three years before going up to university in 1938 I visited Doncaster shed nearly every Sunday. The result of all this was that I missed very few engines which came in or out of works over that period.

I first made regular visits to the various vantage points in 1932, at which time locomotive building at Doncaster was at its lowest ebb on

Following the excitement of its introduction in May 1934 *Cock o' the North* was followed five months later by No.2002 *Earl Marischal, seen here arriving at King's Cross with the 10.15am from Leeds on 5th March 1935.*
(Ken Nunn collection 6386/Locomotive Club of Great Britain)

account of the great trade depression and this nadir of activity was typical of the whole industrial scene. By 1934 there was little improvement, so it was against this gloomy background that there came the news of a great new locomotive type to be built at Doncaster for the Edinburgh–Aberdeen route. Although by that time there were other industries in Doncaster, the Plant was still the most important and as Plant men talked of the parts they were making for the new monster, local pride was thoroughly aroused well before No. 2001 *Cock o' the North* appeared.

As many enthusiasts later knew, the paintshop in the Plant adjoined the works boundary, being separated from it by a high sleeper fence. When I heard that No. 2001 had reached the paintshop, I decided that I must make an effort to look through the windows. Not being sufficiently athletic to stand on my cycle saddle, I went to an adjoining house and asked if I could borrow a pair of steps to look over the fence. The lady was much intrigued and readily obliged. I was somewhat disappointed to find that the view was obstructed. The LNER had withdrawn the GNR 0-8-0s at an early

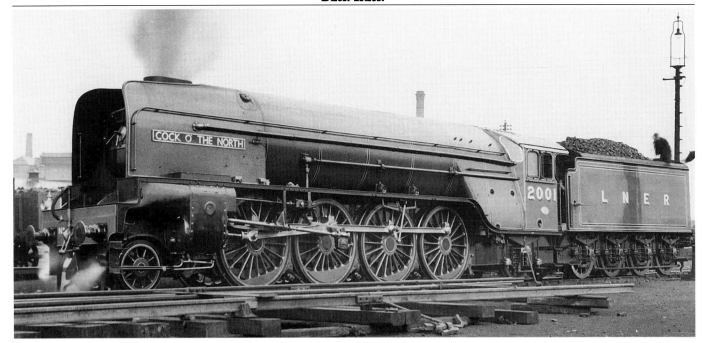

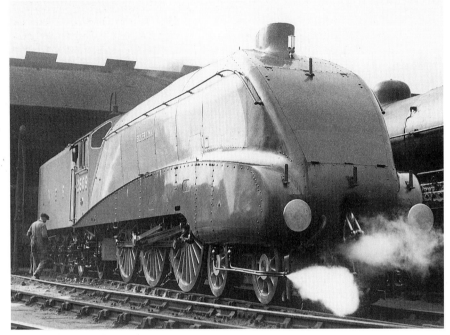

ABOVE: "...Doncaster realised that something novel had emerged from the Plant". The first P2 2-8-2 No.2001 Cock o' the North, which generated such interest on its appearance in May 1934.
(T.J. Edgington collection)

LEFT: Perhaps no new steam locomotive design made a greater public impact than the A4 Pacifics - and in particular the first of them No.2509 Silver Link. Here is the pioneer at King's Cross shed on 21st September 1935. The locomotive was not long out of Doncaster Works and had made its first appearance in London on the 13th, before working the demonstration run of the 'Silver Jubilee' train on 27th September.
(Ken Nunn collection 6521/Locomotive Club of Great Britain)

BELOW: Silver Link speeds past Barkston with the up 'Silver Jubilee', possibly the return working of the publicity run on 27th September 1935. Three days after that the 'Silver Jubilee' went into regular service with only No. 2509 available to haul it for the first two weeks, which it did successfully until the second A4 was ready.
(T.J. Edgington collection)

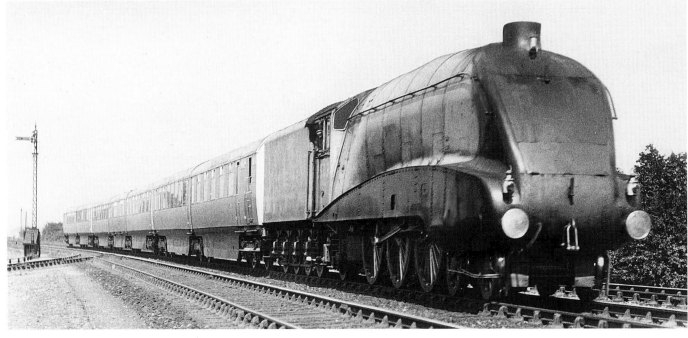

age and their tenders had been preserved for possible re-use. The first two roads in the paintshop were occupied by these tenders, but through the gaps between the tenders No. 2001 could be seen quite clearly. Little information had been published about the engine, so it came as a great surprise to see the shape of the front casing.

A few days later the engine was in steam and it was then that Doncaster realised that something novel had emerged from the Plant. It is difficult now to appreciate the interest, bordering on excitement, that a new locomotive could arouse in the general public. Nothing like the chime whistle had ever been heard there and in those days of relatively low traffic noise, it could be heard all over the town. The *cognoscenti* patted themselves on the back with civic pride, whilst the uninformed sought an explanation, one idea being that a tug boat had strayed up the Sheffield and South Yorkshire Navigation, something which was quite impossible at that time.

For several weeks *Cock o' the North* was based in Doncaster, either back in works or at the Carr Loco (as Doncaster shed was always known). During the construction of the engine, the LNER had sold the photographic rights to a press agency and photography of the engine before its official appearance was strictly forbidden, but the press agency did its work well and the engine had excellent coverage in both the popular and technical press. With the Pacifics daily achieving new levels of performance, no-one doubted that No. 2001 would be a winner.

My first rude awakening came when I encountered F.H. Eggleshaw, the Locomotive Works Manager, near the station one day and made some appreciative remark about his latest product. He replied that it would never be efficient because of the large clearance volume in the cylinders (this was due to the large poppet valves and was, in fact, a contributory factor to the engine's high coal consumption). The subsequent sad history of this class is well known, but for several year No. 2001 was a notable item in any LNER exhibition.

'Railway Exhibitions' were an LNER speciality; they were public relations exercises which raised money for railway charities. They were commonly held in the goods yard adjoining a station, but in May 1934 Doncaster loco works yard was used for one. There was an assembly of newly-painted engines, of which *Cock o' the North* was the showpiece, together with various items of rolling stock and road vehicles, plus side shows for the entertainment of the children. A very popular attraction was the Doncaster 45 ton breakdown crane, lifting a brick container (an open box) in which the public were taken for 'rides' up into the air and round about.

The exhibition occupied the area between the Crimpsall repair shop and the Paint Shop, but no part of the works buildings was open (but lying on the ground one could see under the Crimpsall doors). As the area was criss-crossed by rails, someone had the bright idea of covering the ground with a layer of running shed ash up to rail level, but as it turned out to be a dry and windy weekend, the strongest recollection which many Doncaster wives had of the exhibition was the extraction of large quantities of fine ash from clothing. Needless to say, the railway enthusiasts were there for the whole

time the exhibition was open.

Nos. 2001 and, later in the year, 2002 kept up the excitement until November 1934, when there came the first of the spectacular test runs which preceded the introduction of the 'Silver Jubilee'. A friend whose father was in Doncaster Control showed me the schedule of the train at lunchtime on the day of the run, but the return train was in school time. However, I was more fortunate in seeing the second of the tests, with No. 2750 *Papyrus* in the following March. By then it had become known that a high-speed train between King's Cross and Newcastle was to be introduced in the autumn of 1935 and that a new engine and train would be built for the service.

Very soon our friends in the works began to see parts being made and for the first time we heard the classification A4. Whilst we had no doubt that the A4 would be a great engine, we could not foresee that it would be one of the great engines of all time.

Spring 1935 brought a surprise - an open day at the Plant on Whit Saturday, a very welcome novelty. The fraternity duly appeared, queuing for opening time, armed with sandwiches for the day. To our surprise we found that there was to be an opening ceremony, with Mr. H.N. Gresley welcoming the visitors to his works (did any other Chief Mechanical Engineer ever open an Open Day?). Now came the big question. During the construction of No. 2001, under the agreement with the press agency, no visitors had been allowed in E2, the New Erecting Shop (Doncaster was unusual in still having a separate shop for new construction). We knew that No. 2509 was set up in E2 - was a ban in force again? We hurried to E2 and to our delight found the door open. But now there came to me a disillusionment. At that time our ideas of streamlined engines were based on the German 05 4-6-4s with 7ft 6in driving wheels and with gay disregard for the problem of fitting in the boiler over wheels greater than 6ft 8in in the British loading gauge. I assumed that the new flier would have 7ft+ wheels. Measurement of the frame of No. 2509 showed that its wheelbase was exactly the same as the existing Pacifics so that, at the most, the A4 driving wheels could only be about 2in larger. Indeed the only noticeable difference was in the shape of the front of the framing. Until the 'Silver Jubilee' demonstration run of 27th September 1935, there was thus a slight touch of anti-climax for me in the A4.

At that stage there was only the framing to see, so we had no idea of the actual shape of the engine until it emerged in the first week in September. My introduction to it was unexpected. After returning home from a holiday on a Sunday, I went on a round of all the standard vantage points on the Monday morning. This included Kirk Street, at the end of which was a gate opening into the works yard between the paintshop and the Crimpsall. This gate was normally opened only at starting and finishing times; at other times one looked through gaps and knot-holes in a sleeper fence. But on this occasion the gate was open and there was No. 2509 being propelled into the paintshop. After the pictures of the bulbous German engine, the full side view of an A4 in plain grey all over came as a shock - another touch

of disillusionment.

A few days later No. 2509 appeared from the paintshop and, after inspection by Miss Violet Gresley, returned for some very effective alterations to the boundary between the shades of grey at the front. Next came its trial trips, during which it could be seen standing adjacent to the main line at the old weigh house. Then the news spread through local railway circles that the complete train would have its first trial trip on the following Sunday, leaving Doncaster station at 2.30pm. A great crowd gathered and was rewarded by the sight of the hierarchy of the CME's department, most of whom seemed to be in a state of great agitation, but amongst whom Gresley stood out, a tall, imposing figure - clearly the "boss" and as calm as the proverbial cucumber. Off they went, to the accompaniment of chime whistling, a sound which was now to be heard daily and not just when a P2 was visiting the Plant.

Over the next three years we had continuous excitement, with the successive liveries of the A4s, the 'Coronation' and 'West Riding' trains, and the V2 2-6-2 (which I first saw through the paintshop windows). The changes of livery were particularly noteworthy, as the basic LNER liveries had remained unchanged, apart from the position of lettering and numbering, since soon after grouping and the idea of grey and blue engines seemed quite revolutionary.

In 1938 I went to university and thereafter my observations at Doncaster were intermittent, but there was one notable occasion. One December day in 1940, just before 5.00pm, I was standing on Hexthorpe Bridge (the first overbridge south of the station) when suddenly I noticed a column of smoke rise from the works. From my position it could have been from the Locomotive Drawing Office or from the carriage works behind. Soon flames appeared, but I had to leave as the lighting on my cycle did not conform to the blackout regulations and I had to get home for tea (Summer Time was in force, so dusk in December was at 5.00). After tea I walked to the North Bridge and as I approached the town centre it was clear that there was a great conflagration. The railway works, like many industrial installations, was surrounded by smoke producers. These were cannisters which stood at intervals at the roadside and which, when lit, produced clouds of oily smoke. This was the only time I saw the Doncaster ones used.

When I reached the bridge, I saw that the whole of the main carriage shop was ablaze, but over it was a pall of smoke, partly from the fire but partly from the smokescreen. A little later, by which time I was reporting to a friend at his home, the sirens sounded and aircraft were heard. Doncaster was in great peril and in due course some bombs were heard. However, the smokescreen had worked and the glow of the fire had evidently appeared about a mile north of the works, unless the bombs were very badly aimed.

I relate this story partly because one writer, at least, has recorded that the fire was due to enemy action. Amongst partly-completed coaches which were destroyed in the fire was a new dynamometer car, for which a replacement was made after the war. Later in the war, a fire in the West Carriage Shed, also unconnected with enemy action, destroyed one of the 'Coronation' twin sets which were stored there.

East Midlands Coal Traffic

in LNER Days

by Lawson Little

In 1946, some 60 loaded coal trains were being despatched each day over LNER metals in the East Midlands area - equivalent to an annual traffic in excess of nine million tons. These trains were worked exclusively by locomotives from Langwith and Tuxford sheds and represented the LNER's share of the output of sixteen collieries, as follows:

Colliery	Served by	Notes
Arkwright	LNG	Worked by Markham Junction Pilot
Bilsthorpe	TUX	
Blidworth	LNG	
Bolsover	LNG	
Clipstone	TUX	Worked by Markham Junction Pilot
Creswell	LNG	2 Pilots: 8.35am to 7.00pm / 8.00pm to 12.30am
Mansfield (Crown Farm)	TUX	2 Pilots: 7.01am to 9.25am / 9.21am to 5.15pm
Markham	LNG	
Ollerton	TUX	
Oxcroft No.3	LNG	Worked by Markham Junction Pilot
Rufford	LNG	
Sherwood	LNG	
Shirebrook	LNG	
Thoresby	LNG	
Warsop Main	LNG	Via running powers over LMS line
Welbeck	LNG	

Note that Langwith Colliery is not included; presumably its output was being entrusted wholly to the LMS at this period. All the collieries listed, apart from Arkwright, were served by both LNER and LMS (the LMS reached Thoresby by running powers over the LNER branch).

Study of the Working Timetables for the immediate post-war period can be very frustrating - despite the wealth of detail, some information is noticeable by its absence! For example, the WTT carefully lists all the pilot engines supplied by Langwith and Tuxford (pilot engines being defined as those which are not booked to haul specific timetabled trains. ie shunting and trip working). The Ollerton Colliery Pilot, as an instance, is listed as arriving at the mine on the 7.45am ex-Tuxford West, then working as required before returning home on the 9.40pm to Tuxford North - yet neither of these trains, nor any details of the trip workings between Ollerton and Mansfield or Warsop, are mentioned in the main timetables! This must have made life very confusing for the signalmen!

The reason is, of course, that such workings were 'at the discretion of Control' and would vary according to the output of individual collieries and the state of the market (though in 1946 there was a ready sale for every ton of coal produced).

What the WTT does reveal is the movement of the coal once it had reached the nearest marshalling yard, or concentration sidings as they were called locally. There were two such yards serving the area, Mansfield (actually sited at Clipstone, some four miles north of the town) and Warsop; these were referred to by railwaymen as 'The Con.' and 'The Loops' respectively.

Looking at the accompanying sketch map, one would imagine that logically, all traffic for the west would start from Warsop and that for the east and north be dealt with at Mansfield, but in fact this was not the case, both yards despatching loaded trains in all directions. This was not an oversight by the LNER, but was necessary because of the varying quality and combustion characteristics of coal from each colliery (or even from different seams in the same mine). A breakdown of sales from the East Midlands Area is as follows:

Gas Production	8.6%
Electricity Generation	24.0%
Railways	8.2%
Coke Manufacture	4.9%
Iron & Steel Industry	4.9%
Engineering Industry	2.8%
General Industrial Use	16.6%
House Coal	21.8%
Export and Bunkering	1.4%
Misc.	6.8%

(These figures apply to 1951 but are broadly applicable to earlier years, the 'Dash for Gas' and railway dieselisation still being well in the future).

Most coal traffic in 1946 was moved on Class C trains (though higher-class trains could be made up with coal tonnage if necessary) and these would be hauled by Langwith/Tuxford engines of the following types:

Load Class 3	:	J11
Load Class 6	:	K3, Q1
Load Class 7	:	O4
Load Class 8	:	O2

Maximum train weights were laid down for each load class on every route, these being the tonnage which the specified locomotive would be capable of restarting and moving on the most severe adverse gradient on that route. Details are given in an appendix, the tonnages being expressed in terms of the number of standard coal wagons (ten-ton capacity with a six-ton tare weight) - conversion tables were provided to allow staff to make allowances for other types of wagon.

The two yards at Mansfield and Warsop shared the work more or less equally, with 28 trains from Warsop and 32 from Mansfield, though not all ran every day, of course. In later

04/7 2-8-0 No.63634 passes Clipstone Sidings signal box with a coal train on 18th February 1950. (J. Cupit)

Atlantic

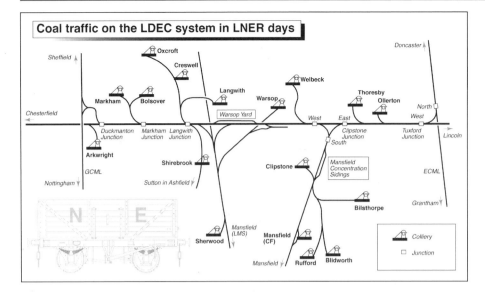

Coal traffic on the LDEC system in LNER days

years the relative importance of Warsop would diminish, but the 'Loops' had the last laugh – at the time of writing they are still in (limited) use, whereas the Mansfield site is a wasteland of ashes and scrub.

In 1946 Warsop despatched seventeen trains eastbound, the breakdown being Whitemoor four, Tuxford or Lincoln seven, Hull/Frodingham/Grimsby four and Woodford two. Westbound there were two trains to Retford (via Worksop), one to Staveley, three to Mottram and five to the Sheffield area yards, a total of eleven.

Mansfield sent out almost all its loaded tonnage northwards, with 21 trains turning east at Clipstone for destinations at Tuxford (five), Lincoln (four), Whitemoor (four), New England (three) and Hull/Frodingham/Immingham/Grimsby (five) and Sheffield (one) while there was a Monday-only train to Warsop, presumably a stock-balancing movement. Only four trains headed south from Mansfield, all to Annesley except one which ran on Tuesdays and Thursdays only to Colwick.

It is interesting to note that anyone describing the traffic in, say, 1926 would list exactly the same locomotives (and a good proportion of the wagons) as would be seen twenty years later. Indeed, the locomotives, with yet another change of ownership painted on their tenders, would continue for a further twenty years after 1946 – no wonder that in those early post-war years we thought everything would go on in the same way for ever! (see Postscript).

The mention of wagons reminds me that in 1946 almost all coal was carried in wooden wagons, the majority being 10/12 ton capacity vehicles previously owned by the colliery companies. The LNER itself had some 71,500 mineral wagons in 1947, with an average age, taking the fleet as a whole, of over sixteen years, so there must have been a number of pre-grouping examples still in service. Production of the well-known steel 16-tonners had started in 1945, to which could be added the similar tapered-side versions built during World War II for the Ministry of Transport, but my recollections of days spent watching the shunting in Newton's Yard at Langwith Junction do not include the sight of more than a handful of such wagons.

Appendix 1: Loaded Departures ex-Mansfield 'Con'., Winter 1946

Tuxford North	am: 12.57 (MX)
	pm: 12.34, 7.40, 7.53, 8.37*
Hull	am: 4.51 (MX), 8.10 (MO)
Lincoln Holmes Yard	am: 7.40
Lincoln Pyewipe	pm: 5.35, 7.27, 10.45
Immingham or Grimsby	am: 10.37
	pm: 12.10
Rotherwood	am: 8.50
Frodingham	pm: 5.08
Whitemoor	am: 3.20, 3.50 (Q)
	pm: 1.45, 9.49 (Q)
New England	am: 2.00, 9.38
	pm: 10.05
Mottram	am: 3.20 (MX), 5.00 (MX), 6.55 (MX), 10.10
	pm: 11.15 (SX)
Warsop	am: 7.55 (MO)
Annesley	am: 1.34, 7.15 (MWFO)
	pm: 6.08
Colwick	am: 7.15 (TuThO)

*or to Pyewipe

Appendix 2: Loaded Departures ex-Warsop 'Loops', Winter 1946 Eastbound

Whitemoor	am: 1.03, 3.17 (MO), 4.00 (Q)
	pm: 11.20 (SX)
Lincoln Holmes	am: 12.20 (SX), 1.30 (MO)
Lincoln Pyewipe	am: 11.40
	pm: 2.40, 3.10
Tuxford North	pm: 12.05, 6.57
Frodingham	am: 10.39
	pm: 4.55 (MWFO)
Hull	am: 9.10 (Q)
Grimsby	pm: 3.30
Woodford	am: 8.00
	pm: 5.22
Westbound	
Retford	am: 1.15 (MX), 6.00 (MO)
Mottram	am: 1.30 (MO), 3.48 (MO)
	pm: 1.58
Sheffield	am: 6.25
	pm: 5.50
Ickles	am: 9.00
Rotherwood	pm: 12.05
Rotherham Road	pm: 8.10
Staveley	pm: 1.20

Appendix 3: Maximum Train Loads (Loads/Empties)

Route	Load Class 3	Load Class 7	Load Class 8
Langwith Junction - Sheffield	40/76	55/100	60/100
Markham Junction - Warsop	33/64	45/83	50/92
ditto piloted to LJ	+5L	+13L	+18L
Mansfield - Lincoln			
Warsop - Lincoln	38/72	58/100	68/100
Warsop - Mansfield			
Colliery Branches:			
Rufford (20mph max)	56/56	67/68	70/74
Blidworth	56/50	67/50	70/50
Clipstone	20/55	26/60	30/66
Bilsthorpe	31/56	44/68	48/74
Thoresby	not quoted	65/45	not quoted
Sherwood	40/50	55/50#	not quoted
Shirebrook	40/50	not quoted	not quoted
Welbeck	30/45	38/55	41/60

May be increased to 55E with approval from LMS control. All loads quoted are expressed as numbers of ten-ton

Postscript

As mentioned earlier, the methods used for handling coal traffic in the area continued unchanged for almost 70 years. Although strictly speaking not relevant to LNER days, it is thought that a few paragraphs detailing the changes which finally took place in 1962 will complete the overall picture.

The position as regards local collieries had by that time changed little since 1946. The severing of the Chesterfield - Lincoln line by the closure of Bolsover Tunnel in 1951 had isolated the mines at the western end of the line (Arkwright, Bolsover and Markham) from the rest of the system, the last years of these collieries being served either via Duckmanton Junction and the former GC Main Line, or where they existed by outlets to the London Midland Region. Oxcroft was no longer in production and Sherwood's output had also been lost to the Midland Region; however, Langwith coal was again coming to Warsop yard. Most of the mines in the Mansfield area were 'million-tonners', the only significant exceptions being Langwith (650,000 tons per annum), Blidworth (800,000) and Thoresby (500,000).

According to a contemporary account, the work of the Warsop and Mansfield Yards had been rationalised, with the former taking coal from Langwith, Creswell, Shirebrook and Warsop collieries, and Mansfield the remainder. Hence the number of loaded trains from Mansfield was now 35 (not all daily) whilst those from Warsop had dropped to sixteen.

The first significant change in handling the coal traffic since 1896 finally occurred when the winter timetable was introduced from 10th September 1962. By this time a large number of new Brush Type 2 (later Class 31) 1,365hp diesels were becoming available and twelve of the Sheffield Darnall allocation were sub-shedded to Langwith. For a very short time they came to the steam shed at Langwith Junction for minor attention, but this arrangement, involving repairs in the semi-roofless carriage shed and refuelling from adjacent rail tankers, was obviously unsatisfactory given the filthy and rundown conditions there and the disused goods shed at Shirebrook Midland was hastily converted into a makeshift depot.

The old Midland-built stone shed was hardly ideal for its new purpose, being able to accommodate only one Type 2 at a time, but a pit was dug out for the fitters' use, along with high-level staging. Later, bulk fuel storage facilities (and eventually a purpose-built maintenance depot) were provided.

The working of coal trains, particularly

Atlantic

RIGHT: *J39 0-6-0 No.64725 and 02 2-8-0 No.63983 climb the 1 in 100 bank between Clipstone West Junction and Welbeck Colliery Junction with a coal train from Clipstone concentration sidings to Mottram on 15th April 1950.* (Author)

CENTRE: *A pair of 2-8-0s, 04/3 No.63732 and 04/8 No.63893, on the Bilsthorpe Colliery branch on 22nd May 1965.* (Author)

BELOW: *J11 0-6-0 No.64299 heads a coal train through Kirkby-in-Ashfield on 2nd May 1953.* (Author)

along the Clipstone - Lincoln line, was becoming a considerable headache to the operating authorities by this time. The steam locomotives were life-expired and generally unreliable and timings on the congested line meant that crews had to be relieved at Lincoln to keep within the normal working day.

The introduction of diesel power, whatever enthusiasts thought about it, was instrumental in transforming the situation. By being able to run at higher speeds and with minimal turn-round time, it was found possible to work trains between Warsop or Mansfield and either Whitemoor, New England or Grimsby with a single crew, out and back in a single shift. To achieve this, the Class 8 timings were replaced by a new Class 7★; the time allowed for a trip, say, to New England, which with steam had taken just under six hours, was now reduced to just over three. This acceleration was aided by the ability to run direct via Sleaford; previously the slow progress south east from Lincoln had necessitated trains being routed via Boston and Spalding to keep out of the way of faster traffic.

The twelve new diesels were intensively rostered, each covering around 2,000 miles every week (equivalent to some three return trips every day) and including a weekly visit to Sheffield for servicing (only minor attention - lubrication checks, brakes etc - was performed at Shirebrook). Loaded trains were standardised at 39 16-tonners plus brake van and were required to run at 35mph - the Type 2s could pull the tonnage at this speed, but soon found difficulty in stopping it! This problem was ingeniously solved by arranging for four vacuum-braked coal wagons ('Minifits') to be marshalled at the front of each train, it being found that their braking effort added to that of the locomotive was sufficient to control the train.

The 'Minifits' were used to carry coal to cement works at Foxton, Cambridgeshire (for Whitemoor trains) and Halling, on the Southern Region (for New England traffic), returning empties being collected and worked in solid fully-braked trains at Class 4 speeds each day. Because the Grimsby traffic covered a shorter distance, no special arrangements were necessary for the 'Minifits' on this route.

A total of 136 trains was worked each week under the new system, 57 to Whitemoor, 35 to Grimsby/Immingham and 44 to New England. The twelve diesels replaced 29 steam locomotives and 26 sets of men were released to meet staff shortages elsewhere.

The new system worked well and only became redundant with the more recent sweeping changes to the whole concept of moving coal from mine to power station using merry-go-round trains. And that, of course, is another story.

(My special thanks to Ted Summerfield, erstwhile member of the freight Train Planning Section at King's Cross, for assistance with the Postscript).

No. 2800 Sandringham passing Stratford with an express on 12th August 1933. Compared with the earlier view, the locomotive now has the number on the cab sides and is still well burnished and polished by Stratford shed.

Darlington-built No. 2811 Raynham
Liverpool Street to Cromer train on 4t.

B17 class 4-6-0 No. 2802 Walsingham of Stratford shed near Chadwell Heath with a Parkeston to Liverpool Street express on 25th May 1929.

The pioneer of the class and pride of Stratford shed, No. 2800 Sandringham waits to depart from Liverpool Street with the 'Clacton Pullman' on 22nd September 1929.

chester with

EARLY YEARS
of the
'SANDRINGHAMS'

by Peter Paye

In 1926 the position of express passenger power on the Great Eastern section of the LNER was critical. New and heavier vacuum-braked coaching stock had been introduced on the Parkeston Quay boat trains and the Southend services and there was a desperate shortage of suitable motive power. The position was partially eased by the transfer of ex-Great Northern Class K2 2-6-0 tender locomotives but they were not particularly suited for the heaviest workings and in the winter after the General Strike, Southend and Cambridge line train service punctuality collapsed. LNER management was stirred into action by the adverse publicity and Gresley was asked to provide a new 4-6-0 class to supplement the ex-GER B12 4-6-0s on the heavier diagrams.

Initial drawings were prepared at King's Cross, but Gresley was not satisfied with the drafts and sent details to Doncaster so that detailed arrangements could be prepared for submission to the Civil Engineer. The specification was for a three-cylinder 4-6-0 tender locomotive with a maximum axle loading of 17 tons to suit the GE route availability but, try as they might, Doncaster Works could not produce within the criteria and the contract for design and initial construction was subsequently awarded to the North British Locomotive Company. The LNER Locomotive Committee had also stipulated a design of locomotive that had as widespread availability as the ex-GE B12 class. However, when the order for ten locomotives, priced at £7,280 each, was placed with the Hyde Park Works on 17th February 1928, the directors had to accept a locomotive with 18 tons axle loading and a much reduced route availability. Before the first ten were ready for traffic, Darlington Works was given an order to build a further twelve, followed in December 1929 by another fifteen.

The new class was to be named after stately homes located on the LNER system and the company officials obtained the permission of King George V to name the initial locomotive *Sandringham* after his country house in Norfolk. The engines were numbered in the series from 2800 and were painted in the LNER green livery with black and white lining. On release to traffic in November and December 1928 the engines were run-in from Eastfield shed, Glasgow, before travelling south to take up duties on the GE section. All were initially allocated to Stratford, except No. 2802 which was allocated to the ex-GCR shed at Gorton for working the 'North Country Continental' boat train between Ipswich and Manchester Central. Within weeks Nos. 2803/4/5 were re-allocated to Parkeston and Nos. 2806/7 to Ipswich, whilst No. 2802 returned to Parkeston and

No. 2814 **Castle Hedingham** *speeds through Shenfield with a Liverpool Street to Norwich express on 29th August 1931.*

then Stratford and was replaced at Gorton by No. 2809.

By Monday 2nd January 1929 there were enough locomotives available to regularly diagram the class to GE section main line express duties, where they replaced the 'Claud Hamilton 4-4-0s and the K2 2-6-0s. They proved popular with footplate crews and appeared to be masters of most work allocated to them. The next five engines on release from Darlington Works between August and October 1930 were dual-fitted

with vacuum and Westinghouse brakes. They were allocated to Stratford, whilst the sixth, No. 2816, was sent to Gorton where it replaced No. 2809. This locomotive and the subsequent build has steam and vacuum brakes. Nos. 2817 to 2819, introduced into service in November 1930, all went to Cambridge whilst Nos. 2820 and 2821 were allocated to Ipswich. Thus by the early 1930s the B17s were gradually taking over all main line services on the former GE section. A further fifteen of the class

numbered up to 2836 appeared in 1931 to strengthen their hold in East Anglia and permitted the transfer of several B12 class 4-6-0s to the Great North of Scotland section. Finally, it is interesting to note that No. 2815, later 1615 and 61615, was allocated to Stratford throughout its lifetime (from 1945 rebuilt as a two-cylinder Class B2), whilst sister locomotive No. 2817, also rebuilt as a B2 and renumbered 1617 and later 61617, was always allocated to Cambridge.

KING'S CROSS
for the NORTH

Photographs by **JOHN EDGINGTON**

Opened on 14th October 1852, King's Cross is not a gem amongst London's termini. Undoubtedly overshadowed by the soaring extravagence of next-door St. Pancras, its dismal yellow London stock brickwork does little to inspire but behind the front screen its two train sheds are quite elegant. Lewis Cubitt was the architect and produced for the Great Northern Railway, a company not known for its architectural frivolity, an economical terminus. John Betjeman wrote "Of all London's termini, King's Cross is the least pretentious. It is an engineering job." Yet if it lacked grace (as it still does in its passenger facilities), it has never lacked importance as the gateway to the East Coast Main Line.

ABOVE: *Many of the empty stock trains in and out of King's Cross were worked by GNR/LNER N2 0-6-2Ts. Here is No.69538 on such a duty during the summer of 1962.*

RIGHT: *The front screen of King's Cross in July 1972. The shambles of buildings which had sprung up in front of the station – railway offices, cab shelters, the Piccadilly tube station, shops (together described by George Dow as an "African village") – had been demolished and redevelopment was in progress from which a then modernistic front canopy and taxi waiting area would emerge (oh good!). The tower contains Frederick Dent's turret clock as displayed at the 1851 Great Exhibition. Black taxis and a Routemaster bus set the London street scene.*

ABOVE: *Edmund Denison, GNR chairman, told shareholders that King's Cross was "the cheapest building for what it contains and will contain that can be pointed out in London" – and this in response to accusations of extravagence! A3 4-6-2 No.60062* Minoru *has arrived at the old Platform 4 (now 3) with an up express in June 1963.*

BELOW: *Before a more sensible redesignation of the platforms was carried out some years ago, uninformed passengers were apt to be confused by the absence of Platforms 3 and 9, both lost during expansions of the internal layout in the 1930s. However, the place to be for observers of King's Cross activity was the end of Platform 10 and on a summer evening in 1962 they had gathered – spotters and briefcase-carrying commuters alike – to watch A1 Pacific No.60120* Kittiwake *leave with an express for Leeds Central. As usual, a spot of wheelslip accompanies the locomotive's departure towards the blackness of Gasworks Tunnel from which an A3 has emerged to back on to its train.*

THE LNER
in colour

Archive photographs from the Colour-Rail collection

ABOVE: *When the B1 mixed traffic 4-6-0s were introduced in 1942, unlined black was the only livery on offer but after the war the LNER managed to turn out a good many in its revived apple green. No.1134, built by the North British Locomotive Co. in March 1947, is seen at Elgin depot in 1948.*
(J.M. Jarvis/Colour-Rail NE33)

RIGHT: *D16/3 4-4-0 No.8840 at Peterborough East in June 1937. Originally Great Eastern Railway Class D56 – later LNER Class D15 – No.1840 built in 1906, it was rebuilt in 1935 with a larger round-top firebox boiler into the D16/3 classification.*
(J.P. Mullett/Colour-Rail NE66)

ABOVE: *A gleaming 'Jazzer' – LNER Class K3 2-6-0 of a design which had originated on the Great Northern Railway in 1920. No.1387 is ex-works in lined black livery at York shed in 1938.*
(H.M. Lane/Colour-Rail NE191)

BELOW: *The D49 4-4-0s first appeared in 1927 as a new three-cylinder intermediate express design to replace older types in the Scottish and North Eastern Areas. The D49/2 variation of the class – named after fox-hunts – had rotary cam-operated Lentz poppet valves. No.247 The Blankney is seen in York shed yard in 1938. That particular hunt pursued its quarry in the Lincoln and Newark area.*
(H.M. Lane/Colour-Rail NE185)

51

ABOVE: *A glorious burst of post-war apple green on A3 No.2582* Sir Hugo *at Grantham in August 1946 – the first A3 to return to green livery after the war. It still has its original number but carried this with its newly-applied livery for only two months before being renumbered 83 that October.* (C.C.B. Herbert/NRM/Colour-Rail NE87)

RIGHT: *Nothing better demonstrated the LNER's flair for publicity and contemporary style better than its A4 streamline Pacifics. Their distinctive outline – painted silver grey on the first four, then garter blue with red wheels – was unmistakeable and, of course, they were outstanding performers with speed records and regular long-distance non-stop runs to their credit. For the introduction of the 'Coronation' service in 1937, five A4s were given names of the main constituents of the Empire, to which end No.4489* Woodcock *was renamed* Dominion of Canada *in June 1937 after only a month in service. The bell had been presented by the Canadian Pacific Railway and was fitted in March 1938 when this photograph was taken outside the Doncaster Works paintshop.* (FNRM/Colour-Rail NE148)

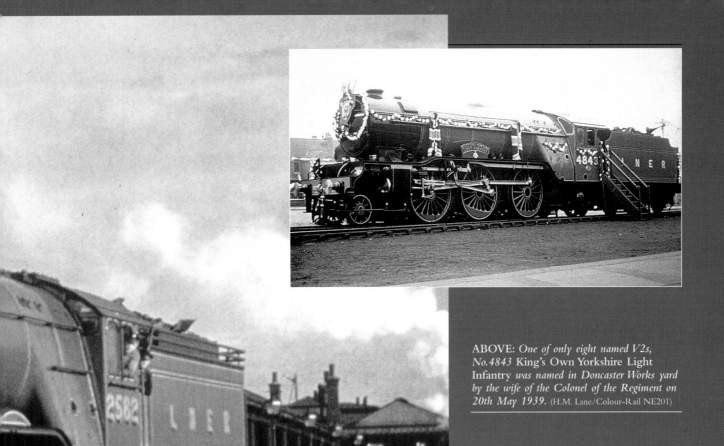

ABOVE: *One of only eight named V2s, No. 4843 King's Own Yorkshire Light Infantry was named in Doncaster Works yard by the wife of the Colonel of the Regiment on 20th May 1939.* (H.M. Lane/Colour-Rail NE201)

BELOW: *In 1903 the North Eastern Railway introduced its Class V Atlantics. The NER worked the East Coast expresses north of York and had tried a 4-6-0 design in 1899, though without conspicuous success. Wilson Worsdell therefore returned to a four-coupled arrangement in the form of a 4-4-2. As LNER Class C6 the locomotives were relegated to less important duties during the 1930s but No. 696 still looks an impressive machine at York shed in 1938. Built at Darlington in 1910, it was withdrawn right at the close of the LNER era in December 1947.* (H.M. Lane/Colour-Rail NE169)

Atlantic

ABOVE: *An evocative view of the platform end at King's Cross looking towards Gasworks Tunnel in 1937. A1 4-6-2 No.2550* Blink Bonny *waits to leave with a train for Leeds and Harrogate. A GNR C1 Atlantic is over to the left in the locomotive yard, with another of that class blowing off in front of the tunnel. The once-familiar King's Cross signal box overlooks the comings and goings.*
(H.M. Lane/Colour-Rail NE150)

RIGHT: *Class J24 0-6-0 No.1956 – a North Eastern Railway stalwart built in 1898 – scampers out of York with a northbound goods in August 1938. The Minster can be glimpsed in the background across the River Ouse which runs below the railway embankment.*
(Colour-Rail NE20)

Notes on the LNER P2 2-8-2s

BY Geoffrey Lund

Geoffrey Lund was an early LNER premium apprentice, commencing at Darlington when Arthur Stamer was Assistant CME to Nigel Gresley. After completing his training in the workshops, he was one of a very few to be awarded a Directors' Scholarship at King's College, London. He spent most of his career in the LNER Locomotive Running Department, at various locations in the North Eastern and Scottish Areas. In BR days, he was responsible for moving the heritage stock from Clapham to the new National Railway Museum at York. Following his retirement, he began to record his memories, but sadly died before he had completed them. Here are his recollections of the P2s, recorded when he was Technical Assistant at Scottish Area headquarters, and later Shedmaster, Haymarket, in the latter years of the war. These notes are kindly provided by his son, Peter Lund.

One of the most controversial aspects relating to the Gresley locomotives hinges around the P2 Mikados built especially for the working of the 'Aberdonian' and other very heavy trains between Edinburgh and Aberdeen. When the P2s started running on the 'Aberdonian', the official maximum load was 530 tons to which can be added at least another 10% for passengers and luggage, so it

was running with nearly 600 tons. The obstacles or limiting factors in the loading were:

1. The start out of Aberdeen at 1 in 96 and the stiff climb to beyond Cove Bay, culminating with a mile of 1 in 102 along the cliffs, prone to very damp and slippery conditions.
2. After the run down to the conditional stop at Stonehaven, on starting from the platform a four mile climb averaging about 1 in 100 with sections of 1 in 85 and 1 in 92.
3. The climb from the stop at Montrose to Usan, on a single line with severe curves at 1 in 88 and continuing at 1 in 111, 3½ miles to the summit.
4. The climb from the permanent speed restriction at Ladybank, 3½ miles at an average 1 in 100 to Lochmuir summit, including over a mile through Falkland Road at 1 in 95.
5. The two-mile climb through two tunnels of 1 in 70, from the severe permanent speed restriction at Inverkeithing to the Forth Bridge

In the down direction the problems were similar except, of course, the two gradients which were the limiting factor on the up, passing Usan and Montrose at 1 in 88, and Forth Bridge North to Inverkeithing, were down grades. The P2s were the solution to these problems – indeed

the maximum loads were probably fixed in the light of the normal loading of the 'Aberdonian', and the locomotives could have taken more, had it been thought desirable.

Much has been said by various knowledgeable writers of the only partial success of the P2s on this route. There are a number of factors which I would stress in the consideration of these locomotives. With particular reference to *Cock o' the North* in its original condition with rotary cam gear, the cylinder design was such that it had a very high clearance volume, twice that of the A4s, and this in itself would account for a higher fuel consumption. Then there was the effect the combination of the rapid-opening exhaust valves and the Kylchap draughting apparatus had on the fire. The smokebox vacuum peaked at so high a value that holes were pulled in the fire and a lot of unburnt fuel was ejected. A third factor was the working diagrams by which the engines operated. In the last years of their life, the engines were divided between Haymarket, Dundee and Ferryhill (Aberdeen), and even with good crews the amount of fire left in the grate at the end of the short runs (Edinburgh to Dundee or Dundee to Aberdeen) meant a lot of unburnt coal. Added to these, the standby losses waiting for the return working could only mean further wasted fuel. Also, there was

The LNER official photograph of No.2001 Cock o' the North *at Doncaster Works in May 1934.*
(The Gresley Society Trust)

No. 2001 fitted with indicating equipment during trials undertaken in June and July 1934. In December the locomotive was shipped to France to visit the locomotive testing plant at Vitry, near Paris.
(Richard Tarpey collection)

Running Superintendent's headquarters at Waverley, in February 1943. One of my jobs there was to examine casualty reports and after coding them according to the part of the locomotive concerned, and the cause, they were entered on the record card for each class of engine.

Engine No. 2001 was undoubtedly a coal eater and following the tests in France it was rebuilt in 1938 with piston valves. However, there were six engines and it was felt that they would get the best attention if they could be allocated to the three depots, Haymarket, Dundee and Aberdeen. The logical plan would have been to put three or four at Haymarket and the remainder at Aberdeen, but Dun-donians are a people no less enthusiastic than the Aberdonians and the staff representatives at Dundee clamoured for their own engines and for the sake of peace got them.

The trains for which the P2s were specially built were the up and down 'Aberdonian' in the height of the holiday season, often duplicated, plus the 10.45 express meat and at least three booked fish trains which at times, particularly during the height of the herring season, were very heavy. There was an old Aberdeen practice which allocated one or more vans to each fish merchant so that the tare load was very high even in off peak times, though the pay load was low. This indeed continued until the early 1950s. The ideal working for the P2 would have been through from Edinburgh to Aberdeen and return with one set of men, but in the days when unions cavilled at any diagrams over eight hours it was difficult and there was never any co-operation with the Operating Department. During my time the 'Aberdonian' left at 7.10pm, due Dundee at 8.53pm. A Class A freight left Stangate Yard at 9.30pm for Aberdeen. I tried, but failed, to get this put back by 20 minutes so that the high-capacity engine could be worked back to Aberdeen instead of lying as it did for twelve hours at Dundee before it worked back. The Operating

trouble from the outset with side rod bushes overheating due to the severity of many curves on the route and I believe the very short and sharp connections in the loco shed yards, particularly from the ashpits at Haymarket. All this must have been appreciated by Gresley in the light of his decision to have the engine undergo exhaustive tests in this country and at Vitry, in France.

Some writers have quoted my old friend Norman McKillop ('Toram Beg'), who wrote unfavourably about these engines. Now Norman was a capable engineman but I think that he misjudged these engines for two reasons.

When the P2s were in their pristine condition he would have been a comparatively young driver and would only have worked them on rare occasions. When he became more senior these engines were being overhauled at Cowlairs and I'm afraid that the standard of work there fell far short of that which obtained at Doncaster or Darlington. True, it was wartime, but the importance of keeping the locomotives in good order could not be got over to the works management. Though I had ridden on the P2s I did not become closely concerned with them until I became Technical Inspector at the Locomotive

Department wanted big engines, but having got them they would not use them effectively. The standby losses in fuel alone with a 50ft grate was a prime cause of the high coal consumption per ton mile, or per mile run, and even with an 8-ton tender, this was not always enough. However, never did these engines have any trouble with any load put behind them. The only congenital design fault was the heating of side rod bushes. This was overcome by giving them larger clearances. As this was something quickly dealt with at the sheds, it was not likely to have incurred more than one day of non-availability. I made a suggestion that the trouble with the side rod bushes could be obviated if a knuckle joint like the B12s had was fitted between the driving and the third and possibly the fourth pair of coupled wheels, but no action was taken.

In May 1942 Edward Thompson went to Edinburgh to arrange a test with the rebuilt W1 4-6-4 to see if a six-coupled locomotive could cope with the heavy Aberdeen sleepers. The result of his visit was that No. 10000 went to Haymarket on 27th May 1942 and stayed until 11th June, working the P2 diagrams. (The rebuilt W1 had an almost identical boiler to the P2/3, No. 2006, which had a longer combustion chamber than the other P2s). The locomotive was considered to have performed satisfactorily and this test then formed the basis of the evidence that a six-coupled rebuild of a P2 would be able to do the same work as the eight-coupled. Unfortunately the six-coupled W1 had only 66 tons adhesion compared with the 80 tons of the original design but as it was early summer when the trial was conducted, the rails were dry and the NE wind was subdued, so evidently no serious slipping occurred.

When it was learned that Thompson proposed to rebuild the P2s, I straight away prepared a memorandum for E.D. Trask, the LRS, setting out the analysis of these for the past twelve

No. 2004 Mons Meg *was completed at Doncaster at the end of July 1936 and for several weeks worked from Doncaster shed before being allocated to Edinburgh Haymarket on 25th August. On 21st August it was photographed departing from King's Cross heading the 4.00pm to Leeds.*

(Ken Nunn collection 6654/Locomotive Club of Great Britain)

months. I recall clearly that of the mechanical failures five out of eight were due to a superheater element blowing out of the header due to them being improperly expanded at Cowlairs, the remainder of the failures being due to side rod bushes. The length of time taken to get the failed engines hauled to Cowlairs and repaired did much to reduce the percentage availability of the class. As there were only six, one out of traffic represented 16⅔% loss of availability. Being only recently appointed to LRS HQ, I was not aware that the die was already cast and that indeed Trask

had written such strong letters to Edward Thompson that Arthur Peppercorn, the Assistant CME, was sent to Edinburgh to tell Trask to stop opposing the CME's intentions.

As for the superheater elements, if the joints are properly made at general overhauls in the works they should last indefinitely if they are tight. In any kind of joint an initial minute leak increases. On the more modern engines, steam pipe joints on to the cylinders and the superheater header are made with 'Lenticular' joint rings to machined faces and seldom give trouble. With the Robinson

No. 2002 Earl Marischal *as rebuilt with A4-style streamlined front-end casing in October 1936.*

(The Gresley Society Trust)

No.2003 **Lord President** *at Dundee Tay Bridge station. It was transferred from Haymarket to Dundee in September 1936.*
(R.S. Carpenter Photos/The Gresley Society Trust)

superheater element which is expanded into the header, no trouble should occur, but where this is not done properly, as occurred on the P2s repaired at Cowlairs, serious and repeated trouble took place. Leakage apart, the elements can be blown out of the header, as happened on the P2s, and this means a very large blow of steam through a 1¼ in diameter hole, which usually causes the engine to become a failure. It should be noted that some writers have spoken of steampipe leaks. I never heard of such a failure, but the bad availability of the P2s in the year prior to the decision by Thompson to rebuild them was

principally due to the superheater element defect for which the engine was sent to the works. The combination of these two problems provided him with the reason for rebuilding, to which must be added his desire to produce his own version of a Pacific, which he was unable to develop as a new express design, under wartime circumstances.

When the P2s were rebuilt, instead of the cylinders being in line with the blastpipe, there was a long fabricated duct from the valve chamber to the centre line of the blastpipe, jointed at one end on to the

cylinder casting, and on the other to to the main frames, which were cut out to allow the exhaust steam to pass through to the blastpipe. From the first day the new engine arrived from Doncaster these joints could not be kept tight and drivers complained continuously that they were driving in a perpetual cloud of steam escaping from them. It was not long before trouble occurred with the (I believe) 8 x ⅞in diameter bolts on either side of the smokebox saddle. These started to fracture and I have myself seen engines of this class on the curved roads leading into the Haymarket ashpits with all bolts fractured and the smokebox cocked up sideways, ⅜in from the saddle. I cannot recall what changes had been made in the securing of the boiler and firebox, but it was evident that the boiler was in fact trying to hold the main frames, bogie and Cartazzi truck rigid, and this trouble continued until they were transferred to the Southern Area, when I lost track of them. A frequent booking by drivers was 'Engine slips badly' (but they would have slipped on Portobello beach!).

In Gresley's day there was a clear recognition that some flexing of the main frames was inevitable. The boiler was secured to the smokebox and this in turn was anchored to its saddle. The controlling forces of the bogie and the Cartazzi truck were carefully balanced, and there was an allowance for expansion of the boiler and the inevitable sideways movement at the firebox end. There was also an intermediate saddle between the driving and trailing coupled wheels, but this did not constrain any movement of the boiler. In consequence fractures associated with the movement of the front end were unknown and leakage from main steampipe joints very rare.

After the engines had been rebuilt as A2s, I made timing tests and unofficial modifications to improve their steaming, wanting the trains on occasions to be made up to 550 or more

tons. I had the weigh bills checked to ascertain the loaded weight. I was horrified to discover that some vans had only a few boxes load and even occasionally an empty van which it had not been possible to shunt out when the loading ceased. At this date the loadings of fish from Aberdeen and the north thereof were down considerably. Apart from the increasing road transport, which was cheaper, a factor in this was that the old cry of 'prime Aberdeen fish' was still used in the markets and this dated from the days when Aberdeen, Peterhead and Fraserburgh were the nearest points to the Dogger Bank and the railway put the fish into Billingsgate for the early morning market. By this time the Dogger Bank was fished out and most Aberdeen fish was the same as came from Hull or Grimsby. The meat, however, was different. It seems to have left Aberdeen at 10.45am way back into history, made up of full loads from Inverness and various places north, and arrived in London before midnight for the Smithfield market. An anomaly which I could never get altered was to run the meat in the same timings as the fish, but I was told that fish vans were coaching stock, while meat was freight. In practice there was no speed limit on either. The meat was all loaded in containers or conflats and it was the commercial aspect which concerned the District Traffic Superintendent, though if you watched the meat going through Stonehaven or Laurencekirk, and saw how the old containers swayed, I am sure the Carriage & Wagon Department would not have been happy to see the times reduced, though the practical change would have been nil.

Comment. *The reference to poor workmanship at Cowlairs during the war years has been mentioned elsewhere, and there are reasons for this: craftsmen would have been diverted to the shipyards, and temporary staff*

No. 2005 **Thane of Fife** *was completed in August 1936 and the 20th was allocated to Dundee. It is seen on the turntable at Aberdeen Ferryhill depot the following year.*
(The Gresley Society Trust)

would not possess the skill and incentive of the regulars. But, especially in view of the importance of maintaining the P2s in good condition, it is a criticism of the supervision and workmanship at Cowlairs to have failed to ensure that the superheater elements were correctly expanded into the headers. Before 1942, the P2s were sent to Doncaster for general repairs, but in the stress of wartime, Cowlairs took over this work, which was not the case in the Scottish-based Pacifics, which continued to go to Doncaster for overhaul. The D11s and D49s repaired at Cowlairs also had Robinson superheaters, *but the superheating arrangements on the P2s were larger and more complex than those on the smaller engines. It would seem that questions could have been asked of the Works Manager and the Area Mechanical Engineer at the time. Also, Thompson's conversion of the class to Pacifics did nothing to alter the superheater arrangements. One wonders whether the problem persisted after rebuilding, as most repairs were carried out at Cowlairs until the engines were sent south in 1950. And finally, do any photographs exist of a failed P2 under tow on its way to Cowlairs for repair?*

The four P2s built in 1936, of which the first was No. 2003 **Lord President,** *appeared with streamlined fronts from new.*
(The Gresley Society Trust)

The three D38 4-4-0s had initially been used on expresses between Aberdeen and Elgin. As built they had eight-wheel tenders with a larger coal and water capacity than any other GNS tender, but later ran with the six-wheel standard version. No.6877 is leaving Aberdeen with a mixed train for Banchory composed mostly of six-wheel stock. The locomotive was withdrawn in 1937. (Atlantic collection)

The Northern Scottish Area of the LNER

Keith Fenwick reviews the fortunes of the former Great North of Scotland Railway system in the post-grouping years

Origins

The grouping of 1923 was preceded by much discussion on the constituents of each of the new companies. At one stage, a single company for the whole of Scotland was actively considered but there was strong opposition from the existing railway companies, who realised there was more sense in amalgamating according to traffic flows. A single Scottish company would not have been financially successful, given some of the sparse areas to be served. This is supported by the high level of subsidy given to ScotRail today but, conversely, ScotRail has demonstrated the advantages of strong local management. In the event, Scotland was to be split between the Eastern and North Western/Midland groups. It was easy to place the three southern Scottish companies, but the Highland and Great North of Scotland Railways were more of a problem. Amalgamation of these two almost happened in 1906, but to put them together with the Eastern group, which would have balanced the two in Scotland, might have been too much of a financial drain. So the Highland went to the LMS and the GNSR to the LNER, separated by 46 miles of LMS line from the rest of its system.

The Great North of Scotland was a product of the 'Railway Mania' of 1845/6. This established many of the Scottish trunk routes, including

the whole of the West Coast Main Line from Carlisle to Aberdeen. The GNSR was set up to continue that route to Inverness by commercial interests based in Aberdeen, in fact the same people who promoted the Aberdeen Railway, the link from the Granite City to the south.

The GNSR was not able to raise any money for a while but eventually amassed enough to build its line as far as Keith. Inverness interests promoted their own line from Inverness to form a junction there, becoming part of the Highland Railway when it was formed in 1865. The divided control of what should have really been one through route was to affect the pattern of services until well in to British Railways days.

The GNSR eventually reached Elgin via Craigellachie in conjunction with the Morayshire Railway and in the 1880s established a third route to Elgin. While the GNSR ran express trains from Elgin by its longer routes, the Highland often preferred to stop its trains at all the intermediate stations on its shorter route. Overall journey times between Aberdeen and Inverness were down to four hours before the First World War, for a distance of 110 miles!

So what the LNER inherited in 1923 was a compact system running from Aberdeen to Keith and Elgin via Craigellachie and via Buckie, with a large number of branch lines. There was the Deeside line, famous because it

served Balmoral, the Buchan line to Peterhead and Fraserburgh which carried large amounts of freshly-caught fish, the Speyside line which served some of the best distilleries, plus minor branches to Alford, Old Meldrum, Macduff and Banff. Off the Buchan line were two more branches, to St. Combs and Boddam. The last-named served the Cruden Bay Hotel, one of three owned by the company, which had a good golf course but little else to attract custom. A short electrified tramway connected the Cruden Bay hotel to the local station. The GNS had developed several bus routes as feeders to its railway services. A number survived to be inherited by the LNER along with a large fleet of buses and lorries.

Locomotive stock consisted largely of 4-4-0s. Apart from a few 0-6-0 and 0-4-4 tanks, plus some 0-4-0 tanks for shunting the harbour lines at Aberdeen, 4-4-0s had been built exclusively for 40 years. Coaching stock was a very mixed bag. There were some respectable modern vehicles but the GNSR positively hoarded old vehicles for use on excursion trains - 'old stock trains' in the terminology of the working notices. The company had been slow to move to six-wheeled and bogie vehicles, building four-wheelers until the mid-1880s and the last six-wheelers in 1916. The oldest vehicle taken over by the LNER was built in 1859 and everything built after 1865 was passed on. Goods vehicles were a similar mixture. To maintain this stock, a new and well-equipped works had been established on a greenfield site at Inverurie, seventeen miles north of Aberdeen,

The early years of the Great North had seen recurring financial problems and it was not until the 1880s that a measure of prosperity was achieved. The company only had three general managers throughout its existence and its chairmen included several capable men. A spirit of innovation can be seen in the adoption of new methods and techniques. Much of the track was single line, so automatic tablet exchangers were introduced. Ballast plough vans were introduced based on the designs introduced on the Great Western. Several stations were rebuilt in granite in an imposing style around the turn of the century and then a major rebuilding was undertaken at Aberdeen, where the Joint station was shared with the Caledonian and North British. The company had even undertaken a detailed study of the economics of each of its lines, giving financial information which was not available to many other railway managements.

The financial results in the last few years of the company's independent existence matched those of many other lines, with a dividend of 3% being paid in most years from 1890 until the grouping. Given that the area served was largely agricultural, with no industry to speak of, this shows the efficiency of the management. The capital of the GNSR at the grouping, and the corresponding LNER stock exchanged, is given on the next page.

GNSR Stock	LNER Stock	Value
4% Lien	4% 1st Guaranteed	£1,230,252
4% Guaranteed	4% 2nd Guaranteed	£363,862
4% A Preference	4% 1st Preference	£593,556
4% B Preference	4% 1st Preference	£405,000
4% C Preference	4% 2nd Preference	£247,737
Ord	5% Preferred Ordinary	£1,295,132
Def Ord 1	Deferred Ordinary	£102,822
Def Ord 2	Deferred Ordinary	£397,396
4% 1891	4% 2nd Pref	£200,000
4% 1894	4% 2nd Pref	£375,000
	Total	£5,210,757

Of the directors at the time of the grouping only one, Alexander Duffus, was elected to the LNER Board[2]. Duffus was an Aberdeen advocate who had been a director of the GNSR since 1915 and became its chairman in 1922. His profession was well represented on the board of the GNSR, so he would have continued a long tradition had he not unfortunately died in 1924.

Takeover

From an organisational point of view, the grouping was a major undertaking. A variety of companies, each with its own management and ways of working, suddenly found everything was changing. Local management was replaced by control from a distance. The LNER adopted a decentralised policy from the start, enabling some local management to be retained in the various Areas. The Great North became the Northern Scottish Area, but in its case what really happened was a takeover by the North British – or the Southern Scottish Area, as it was now known. The General Manager, Scotland – James Calder – had overall charge and some functions were moved away from Aberdeen. The boundaries of the old GNSR were retained unaltered in the NSA, which remained a separate operating district for fifteen years.

At national level, the LNER chairman was William Whitelaw, grandfather of the late Viscount Whitelaw. Whitelaw was a public figure in Scotland with industrial interests who had been chairman of the Highland Railway before taking the same position in the North British, so the decentralised approach to management may have been influenced by his experience in running smaller lines.[3]

Initially, the Northern Scottish Area continued to run many of its own functions, but gradually these were moved south to Edinburgh. Even local allocation of locomotive and rolling stock numbering continued until separate numbering was abandoned on the whole system in the late 1930s.

Using the traditional terms of 'officers' and 'servants', the grouping had a major affect on many of the officers, but meant little to the men, especially in the short term. The work of running the railway had to go on. Transfer around the system, particularly of station staff and anyone at more senior positions, had long been a feature of railway life and now they had to be prepared to move even further. People who had grown up in rural Aberdeenshire found themselves working among the industrial towns of Fife and the Lothians.

Operations

Operationally, north and south of Aberdeen continued to be run on pre-grouping principles. The SSA was responsible for trains from the south into Aberdeen, using running powers from Kinnaber Junction, and its locomotives continued to use the LMS (ex-Caledonian)

TOP: *Maud signal box was the only new one constructed during the LNER period, replacing two separate boxes. It was situated at the south end of the platforms, with a clear view of the goods yard. The design is actually North British (Type 8 of the Signalling Study Group), but granite has been used in its construction where brick would normally have been used. This view dates from 1969, by which time only goods trains operated. However, it was necessary to retain token working to Dyce to enable trains to run to both Peterhead and Fraserburgh each day.* (Keith Fenwick)

LOWER: *Single line instruments in Keith Junction box. This box controlled the double line to Grange and single line to Auchindachy on the Craigellachie route to Elgin by block working and the connection to Keith East box on the Highland by telephone working. As part of the LNER's modernisation of signalling, key token instruments replaced Tyer's tablet instruments to Auchindachy in 1927 and in 1931 long section working was added to Drummuir. This photograph, taken in 1962, shows the Auchindachy key token instrument on the left. On the right is the Tyer's No.6 tablet instrument for long section working to Drummuir. The box above it, to the left, switched between long and short section working.* (Keith Fenwick)

shed at Ferryhill. A scheme to relocate these engines to the ex-GNS shed, at Kittybrewster on the north side of Aberdeen, was examined as early as 1924. Locomotive running matters were initially in the hands of J.P. Grassick, ex-NBR, for the SSA and T.E. Heywood, ex-GNSR Locomotive Superintendent, for the NSA. When Heywood was transferred to Gorton in July 1924, Grassick assumed responsibility for the whole of Scotland and soon wrote to Calder suggesting that considerable economies could be achieved by transferring locomotives from Ferryhill to Kittybrewster. Some subsequent correspondence survives, but nothing to indicate why the scheme was finally rejected. Objections were raised on the grounds that the heavier locomotives used south of Aberdeen would

damage the lighter ex-GNS track and there was even a problem with running engines through the station at Aberdeen which, of course, was still jointly owned by the LMS and LNER. The NBR only ever had running powers and was not a joint owner, so it was judged that running freight engines from the SSA would have to be approved by the Joint Station Committee. The LNER, of course, was perfectly entitled to run its own freight engines off the Deeside line through the station! Some improvements would have been necessary at Kittybrewster to increase its accommodation and there was also a problem that engines would take longer to go to and from Kittybrewster than Ferryhill and also increase train movements within the Joint Station.

Even in BR days both sheds were retained and their responsibilities were never changed. All that happened was the occasional use of Kittybrewster engines to help with workings to the south, usually as pilots.

The impact of road competition led to the closure of some lines. The first to go was the short branch from Aberdeen to Old Meldrum. The road journey to Aberdeen was much more direct, so traffic had dropped off considerably before the line was closed in 1931. This had, in fact, been the first branch to be opened, in 1856. Freight services continued until 1966. Next the Cruden Bay service was

distilleries. One was at Towiemore, near Keith on the Dufftown, and the other at Dailuaine (pronounced 'Daloon'), on the Speyside line. Both had short platforms with wooden edges. Towiemore had an old coach body, dating from the 1860s, as a shelter, but Dailuaine was only equipped with an oil lamp and was accessed only by a footpath.

Rolling Stock

The LNER inherited 493 passenger vehicles and 118 non-passenger coaching vehicles, of which 127 and 69 respectively were dual braked. It was quickly realised that something

scrapped but the bodies were found new uses. Several were retained by the railway, typically as store rooms at stations. The rest were offered to the local farmers, who purchased them for henhouses, etc. Wagon bodies were also sold in this way. Even today, it is possible to roam the farms of Aberdeenshire and find an odd coach body built in the 1870s and withdrawn in the 1920s, together with many built in the 1880s and 1890s. Four and six- wheeled bodies were preferred to bogies, which had to be cut in half to be transported easily. This policy continued until the closure of Inverurie Works. In 1960 coach bodies could still be had for £1 per foot.[4]

Although it never possessed anything larger than a 4-4-0, the Great North is known to have considered a 2-6-0 to satisfy a need for a larger locomotive which was capable of fitting on 50ft turntables. The LNER was faced with satisfying this need after the grouping and did so by transferring locomotives from other Areas. In the earlier years, the choice was restricted by the need for Westinghouse brakes and by the axle load limit. Quite a number of ex-NBR 4-4-0s of Class D31 were transferred starting in 1925. 33 examples of this class saw service on the NSA, with a maximum of twenty at any time. Four D51 4-4-0Ts were transferred from 1926 onwards but these were just as elderly as the Great North engines and had gone by 1933. Several other tank engines were transferred, including NER G5 0-4-4Ts and J72 0-6-0Ts, plus a single N14 0-6-2T from the North British. A Y10 was tried for a short time in 1934 and three F4 2-4-2Ts were transferred from the Great Eastern section to work the St. Combs branch in 1933. Two ex-NBR J36s were tried in 1946 for a short time and Gresley's V4 No.3401 *Bantam Cock* was tried in 1941. The Sentinel railcar *Highland Chieftain* was allocated to the NSA in 1929-30 but was not very successful.

The best-known class to be transferred was the ex-Great Eastern Railway B12s. The first ones were transferred in 1931 and the number gradually rose to 22 at nationalisation. These were well regarded by footplate crews and acquired the nickname 'Hikers'. Argument continues as to the origins of this name – it was either a reference to the ACFI feedwater heaters which marred the smart outlines of the boilers, or else reflected the then current craze for 'hiking'. The same name was later applied to 'Black Fives' on the Highland lines. The B12s handled the majority of the heavier duties until 1946, when B1s started to appear. A total of nine had been allocated to the NSA by nationalisation, the only new locomotives to appear on Great North metals since the last of the D41s (GNSR Class F) in 1921.

Apart from the D31s and B12s, the numbers of each class were small. Locomotive allocation was entirely based on what was seemed to be suitable for the work rather than trying to keep maintenance costs down by collecting all examples of smaller classes in the same locality.

Infrastructure

Investment in the infrastructure was kept to a minimum. Signalling renewals were limited mainly to replacement of lower quadrant arms with upper quadrant ones, when worn out. One new signal box was erected - at Maud, to basically a North British design, to replace two boxes. An experimental Adlake Lebby electric semaphore signal lamp was tried at Kittybrewster

TOP: *Six 0-6-0Ts of GNSR Class D were built by Kitson & Co to a Manson design in 1884. They were used on pick-up freights and on the Aberdeen suburban services from their start in 1887 until the introduction of the Class R 0-4-4Ts in 1893, but later years saw them relegated to local goods and shunting duties. As LNER Class J90, No. 6816 is seen at Kittybrewster; it was scrapped in 1935.* (Atlantic collection)

LOWER: *Three 4-4-0s of GNSR Class Q - LNER Class D38 - were built in 1890 based on the successful Class O (LNER D42) but with a larger driving wheel diameter of 6ft 6½in. No. 6875 stands round the turntable at Kittybrewster shed in August 1932. It was withdrawn at the beginning of 1938.* (Atlantic collection)

withdrawn in 1932, initially for the winter months only, but it never resumed in 1933. This was one of the last lines opened, in 1898, and it had never prospered. Perhaps if it had been extended through to Peterhead it might have had a better time. Again the line remained open for goods, but was progressively closed during the war. Eventually, the track for several miles from Ellon was used for the storage of the large number of wagons which required attention after the war. No other line closures occurred until BR days, but the once-popular Aberdeen suburban services to Dyce on the main line and Culter on the Deeside line were withdrawn in 1937, having lost most of their traffic to local bus and tram services.

Two new halts were opened, both to serve

had to be done to get rid of the oldest. In the first few years, many of the old coaches were scrapped but very few new vehicles, restricted to those for through workings to Inverness, were sent to replace them. Instead the Area had to rely on hand-me-downs. This had to be from areas using the Westinghouse brake for several years and also had to avoid gas-lit coaches since the GNSR had only used oil and electricity. Vacuum brakes became standard in 1928 but changeover on the NSA was deferred, presumably because of its isolated situation. The carriage rosters indicate that full-scale changeover did not take place until 1935. By September 1938 only the St. Combs branch retained Westinghouse-fitted stock. Once withdrawn, coach underframes were between 1932 and 1934. To improve safety, many single line tablet instruments were replaced by key tokens. This enabled intermediate sidings to be released by the key token and several boxes controlling only sidings were replaced by ground frames. GNS practice had been to provide two boxes at most passing loops, because of the distance from the points to the box. In general this was retained, but some loops were altered to be controlled by one box. Long section tokens were added so that some of the lesser-used boxes on the single lines could be switched out. Little was done to the stations, although many wooden footbridges had to be replaced because of rot. The LNER installed a neat design using old rails.

The GNS had opened a new locomotive and carriage works at Inverurie at the turn of the century. This was built on a green field site complete with cottages for workers and communal facilities. New construction of locomotives and rolling stock ceased during 1923 and the works thereafter concentrated on maintenance and repairs. The capacity was such that stock was sent from the SSA, bringing some of the largest engines onto GNS metals. The staff always took a pride in their work which was carried out to a high standard. Even in the 1960s, just before closure, diesel locomotives repaired at Inverurie were more reliable than some from other works.

Train and Bus Services

Changes to train services were very limited; there had been few changes in pre-grouping days so this was not surprising. Just before the grouping, the first restaurant car service had been introduced when the GNSR leased an NBR vehicle to provide breakfast on the morning train from Aberdeen and lunch on the return working from Inverness. A through sleeping car was introduced from London to Elgin and Lossiemouth, although it terminated at Elgin when there were no passengers for Lossiemouth. Lossiemouth was, of course, the home of Ramsay MacDonald, then Leader of the Opposition. He was Prime Minister for nine months in 1924 and then from 1929 - 1935. Initially worked by a first class vehicle, a composite twin was later used after third class sleeping cars were introduced. The return departure was at 4.05pm and this facility continued until 1939.

The NSA was not known for speed, but *Whitaker's Almanack* for 1925 has a curiosity. It carried a table of fastest running trains without stoppage which included the 1.00pm from Aberdeen. This ran non-stop to Auchindachy (between Keith and Dufftown), a distance of 56.8 miles at an average speed of 48mph. The train was actually a Wednesdays and Saturdays excursion to the Speyside line. It was very popular in pre-war days, when the fare was 2s 6d (12½p). The stop at Auchindachy was to cross another train; previously its first stop was Dufftown.

Looking at the general passenger services, little changed until the war. There was no attempt to improve the through services between Aberdeen and Inverness. Some trimming of services did occur, such as reducing a few trains to Saturdays only. Like the rest of the network, services were cut back during the war years and the coal shortages of the late 1940s. Although services were little improved to meet road competition, cheaper fares were offered for day and short period returns. Half-day excursion fares were also introduced.

Sunday services had never been a feature of the Great North but were introduced in the

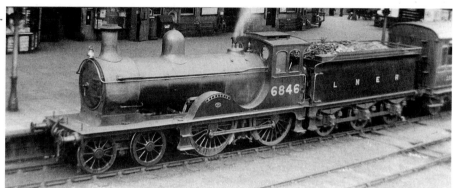

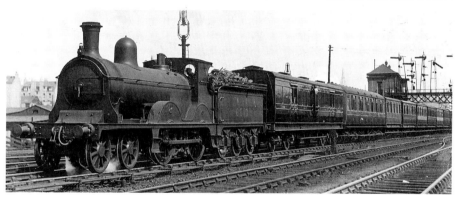

TOP: *During the 1930s and 1940s the mainstay of the motive power on the NSA were the locomotives of Class B12 transferred from the Great Eastern section. As well as being available due to replacement by newer engines, they met the dual requirements of Westinghouse braking and light axle load to work north of Aberdeen. The B12s worked in the area until 1954, by which time B1s had replaced them, In this view, No.1524 leaves Inverurie for the north on 4th April 1947. The locomotive looks very clean in its then new apple green livery hauling a train of Gresley-designed coaches. A couple of six-wheelers of more ancient vintage sits in the bay platform which was one used by the Old Meldrum trains on the far left.* (Jim Jarvis)

CENTRE: *No. 6846* Benachie *was the last of the D40s turned out of Inverurie in September 1941. It was photographed at Elgin on 25th August 1938.* (Atlantic collection)

LOWER: *Class D43 No. 6813 on a train heading for the Deeside line out of Aberdeen. This locomotive, built by Manson in 1890, was rebuilt in 1916 and withdrawn in 1937. The train consists mainly of Great North six-wheelers, but there are two bogie vehicles leading - a GNS full brake dating from 1903 and an LNER corridor.* (F. Moore)

1920s, both on the main line and on Aberdeen suburban services. Later, services were provided to Ballater and Macduff, where a smart new open-air swimming pool, typical of many opened during the 1930s in warmer parts of the country, would have added to the traffic.

Excursion trains had always been a feature on the line, mainly linked to specific holidays. Although the 1930s are the years of depression in

most people's minds, excursions became more widespread and many were operated, some complete with refreshment facilities. The NSA even put in a bid for a complete set of new excursion stock, Gresley's design of steel-sided vehicles with bucket seats, but this was turned down.

The pioneering bus services operated by the GNSR saw many changes. Even before 1923, local competition was being felt and some routes were abandoned. This process continued throughout the 1920s as the railways tried to react to the growing loss of local traffic. The LNER had, of course, inherited the powers to run road motor services which were obtained by the GNSR in 1906[5] but in 1928 the LNER obtained more general powers along with all the other railway companies. This spurred the development of several more services, some parallel to railway lines. For instance, the Braemar - Ballater service which was the first to be operated in 1904, was extended all the way to Aberdeen. Further change followed in 1930, when all the road services were transferred to a reconstructed Scottish Motor Traction Co. (SMT) and operated by its subsidiary, Walter Alexander & Sons of Falkirk. The LMS and LNER between them held 50% of SMT but for all operational purposes they relinquished control of the road operations and there was no attempt at connecting road and rail services.

very much as part of the GNS. One of the Inverurie drawings now held in the Scottish Record Office is for a tongue press for the Palace Hotel and another for modifications to the bain marie!

The hotel at Cruden Bay had been developed at the turn of the century in conjunction with its golf course, to benefit from the popularity of golf at the time. Although it faced south, it was still on the east coast and not many miles from Peterhead, which is nicknamed 'the bloo toon' because it is so cold! The hotel at Cruden Bay remained open until World War II when it was commandeered by the armed forces for hospital use. It never recovered after the war. The golf course is still popular, but all the buildings were pulled down many years ago. To serve this hotel, an electric tramway was constructed from Cruden Bay station on the Boddam branch. After the Boddam line closed to passengers in 1932, a seven-seater

handle wartime traffic from, for instance, the felling of timber on Deeside by Canadian forestry teams and the construction and operation of several airfields on the flat lands of the north east. Operations were initially controlled from Edinburgh, including the allocation of locomotives and rolling stock and no doubt NSA engines would be seen further afield than in peacetime. A dedicated control office was established in Aberdeen in 1943. However, records from these years are few and far between and photographs almost non-existent. Aberdeen suffered some bomb damage, including direct hits on Kittybrewster locomotive and carriage sheds in 1940 and 1943.

LNER staff played a major part in one incident of national importance early in the war. Early on the morning of 30th September 1940, a group of three German spies, Werner Walti, Karl Drucke and Vera Erikson, were landed on the Morayshire coast in choppy waters near Buckie. Their intention was to cycle to London, using English bicycles found in the basement of the British Consulate in Bergen. Unfortunately for them, the bicycles were lost in the transfer from the plane to their dinghy and they were therefore forced to try to travel south by trains. For this, they were not fully prepared.

The party split up, with Drucke and Vera Erikson going west and Walti going east. The former had studied their maps and planned to take a train from Portgordon. Carrying a large suitcase and two smaller bags, they reached the station at 7.30am. They were observed by the station master, John Donald, and the porter, John Geddes. Vera spoke first and asked the name of the station, arousing suspicion. Drucke, meanwhile, pointed out the name Forres on a wall timetable to Donald. As he opened his wallet crammed with notes to pay for two third class tickets, the station master noticed that the bottom of the man's trousers were soaking wet and the woman's shoes were also damp. Telling the porter to keep them talking, John Donald telephoned the local policeman, Constable Grieve. Within ten minutes, Grieve arrived at the station and asked to see their identity cards. He noticed that although both claimed to be refugees, there was no immigration stamp on either card, also that both were written in a Continental style of handwriting.

Grieve took both to the police station and contacted Inspector Simpson at Buckie, who went to Portgordon. Several suspicious items were found on them, including a Mauser pistol loaded with six rounds of ammunition and a wireless transmitter. This led to steps being taken to find out if anyone else had landed. It was then discovered that, earlier that morning, a man had walked into the booking office at Buckpool station. There he had been told by the porter, George James Smith, that the train for Aberdeen had just left and the next one would not call at Buckpool but would leave Buckie at 9.58am. He asked if there was a bus, but the porter did not know, so he walked to Buckie carrying a large brown suitcase and a smaller one. At Buckpool he had tried to purchase a ticket to Perth, but the porter could not find a fare.

After eventually catching the train at Buckie, Walti travelled to Aberdeen and then on to Edinburgh. When he arrived there at 4.30pm, he asked a destination board attendant named Cameron when the next train left for London.

TOP: *Ex-North Eastern No.7287 was one of three Class G5 0-4-4Ts transferred to the NSA during the war. they were used mainly on shunting duties and survived until the early/mid-1950s. No.17287, seen here at Inverurie, lasted until 1953. It is still in wartime black livery with the simplified 'NE'.*

LOWER: *One investment which the LNER did make in locomotive facilities was the construction in about 1935 of a concrete coalaing tower at Kittybrewster, seen here in the background. Vacuum powering for the turntable was also introduced. In the foreground stands Class Z4 No.6844 and D40 No.6845, given consecutive numbers due to the vagaries of the GNS numbering scheme, which mapped directly on to the 1924 LNER renumbering. The photograph is undated, although the Z4 appears to be in post-war green.*

Hotels

The Great North ran three hotels, two in Aberdeen and one at Cruden Bay. The Aberdeen hotels were the Station, still in existence and now incorporating the former GNSR offices which were adjacent, and the Palace Hotel. The latter was the principal hotel in Aberdeen and was situated in Union Street. A direct entrance was provided from the north end of the Joint station. Sadly a fire broke out in October 1941, which badly damaged the building and led to the deaths of six servant girls. The hotel was never reopened. The hotels had been run

Rolls Royce was purchased to carry passengers to either Ellon, the nearest station, or Aberdeen. The tramway continued in use to carry laundry from the hotels in Aberdeen until 1941.

The war years

Unlike the neighbouring Highland section of the LMS, the NSA was not called upon to carry prodigious levels of traffic during the war and additions to facilities were limited to extra siding and refuge accommodation on the main line. Traffic, of course, increased to make up for the lack of road transport and to

Atlantic

He was told it was at 10.00pm and Cameron portered his suitcase to the left luggage office where it was deposited.

The Buckie police contacted Aberdeen police, who confirmed that a man answering Walti's description had travelled south. Meanwhile, the dinghy used to land the trio had been retrieved by the coastguard at Buckie. News of the events reached the Criminal Investigation Department (Criminal Branch) in Edinburgh at 5.10pm and a comb-out of the city was immediately ordered. All the porters at Waverley were questioned, but it was only by chance that the destination board attendant, who should not have been carrying bags, realised that he had met the suspect. As a result, Walti was arrested when he came to retrieve his suitcases later in the evening, although he had to be taken by surprise as he was carrying a loaded pistol in his pocket. He also had a flick knife and almost succeeded in using it; such knives were then unknown in Britain.

All three were taken to London for interrogation. Subsequently Walti and Drucke were sent for trial, found guilty and executed. The Solicitor General prosecuted and the railway staff involved in their apprehension were called to give evidence. Erikson, who turned out to be the leader, was never brought to trial and is believed to have lived on the Isle of Wight after the war.

LNER Legacy

The LNER handed over to British Railways a network which was still run in much the same way as it had been in 1923. Maintenance had suffered because of the war but throughout the period expenditure had been tightly controlled. Staff at rural stations had been reduced in line with declining traffic. Little had been done to adapt to the changing needs of transport - management style had been one of reaction to change, not one of seizing the initiative and taking advantage of the greatly-increased demand for mobility by the public. Not that there was any marked change in this policy in the early years of BR!

The Great North of Scotland Railway Association was formed in 1964 and in those days there were many members who knew the Great North before the grouping and could recall it with affection. Little was said about the years under LNER control, either good or bad. Of course, much of the contemporary discussion was on the effects of the Beeching plan which was to lead to the closure of nearly all the remaining lines in the north east.

What the LNER had inherited in 1923 had, in fact, changed very little over the subsequent 25 years, far less than it had in preceding quarter centuries. The railway served the area as it had done for as long as most people could remember. Many people continued to use it out of habit, especially for freight; it took the railway strike of 1955 to show that life could go on without the railways. In many ways this reflected the remoteness of the Area. The LNER management had much more difficult problems to solve further south, so the NSA could look after itself. This it did with the same quiet efficiency that had been the hallmark of the Great North management in its later years.

References
1. Report to 134th and final Annual General Meeting.
2. Vallance, H A, *Great North of Scotland Railway*.

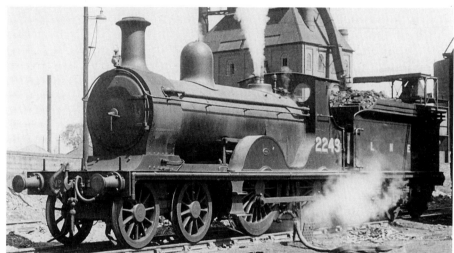

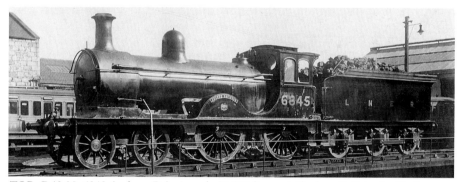

TOP: *D40 No.6848* **Andrew Bain** *in early LNER livery at Aberdeen. Built by the North British Locomotive Co. in 1920, it was renumbered 2276 in 1946 and was withdrawn as BR No.62276 in 1955.* (Atlantic collection)

CENTRE: *The LNER D41 class was the largest taken over from the GNSR. It consisted of GNSR Class S and T which differed only in detail. Seen at Elgin shed in 1947 is No.2243, built by Neilson & Co in 1895 and withdrawn in 1951.* (Atlantic collection)

LOWER: *Class D40 No.6845* **George Davidson** *was dated from 1921, one of the last class of 4-4-0s built for GNSR. As can be seen from this photo taken on the turntable at Kittybrewster, clean engines were still turned out in a respectable condition. These locomotives were painted black from the start, although the preserved* **Gordon Highlander**, *from the same class, has sported Great North green since its restoration in the late 1950s.*

3. Bonavia, *Four Great Railways*, p56.
4. See 'LNER Northern Scottish Area Coaches', by S.C. Carter, *Backtrack* Vol. 13, No. 5, May 1999, for a detailed description of coaching stock in the NSA.
5. Great North of Scotland Railway Order Confirmation Act, 1906, 6 Ed7 c27.

Other sources include the Scottish Record Office, West Register House, Edinburgh and the publications of the Great North of Scotland Railway Association, including *Great North Memories, the LNER Era*. Details of membership can be obtained from R.P. Jackson, Craighall Cottage, Guildtown, Perth PH2 6DF.

LNER COWANS SHELDON
35/6 AND 45-TON
STEAM BREAKDOWN CRANES

by Peter Tatlow

Introduction

Shortly before grouping the Great Northern·and North Eastern Railways had both witnessed the introduction of 4-6-2 Pacific locomotives by Gresley and Raven respectively, later classified A1 and A2 by the LNER. The subsequent multiplication of the former and improvement as A3s, together with the development of the 2-8-2 version for heavy freight trains in the form of the P1s, brought about a requirement to handle loads in excess of 90 tons in the event of a derailment. This need was met in 1926 by the purchase from Cowans Sheldon of Carlisle of two 45-ton steam breakdown cranes (Works Nos. 4524 and 4525), which were allocated to the East Coast Main Lline at Doncaster and Gateshead[1]. North of the border with Scotland the North British had bequeathed a massively-constructed 36-ton crane supplied in 1914, also from Cowans Sheldon (Works No. 3310), stationed at St. Margaret's, Edinburgh. In the days before the Health and Safety Executive breathing down one's neck, I have little doubt it would be used to lift one end of such locomotives when the occasion demanded.

The carriages of all large rail cranes and particularly breakdown cranes are provided either with telescopic propping girders, or vertically hinged outriggers. While travelling in train formation to and from the scene of operations, these are stowed within the loading gauge. On site, the lifting capacity of the crane is severely restricted by the possibility of overturning when supported only by its running wheels set at the distance apart of the rails at approximately 5ft. Whilst

stationary, the crane's performance can be significantly improved, however, by drawing out the propping girders, or swinging out the outriggers and wedging, or jacking, on a firm support to increase the propping base. Until recently British practice has invariably been to adopt propping girders, due to the restrictions of the loading gauge, rather than the outriggers common overseas. Two or three pairs of girders are usually provided and should be drawn out and supported on both sides. Such cranes are also equipped with rail clips, but these are of little use on large cranes because any tendency to uplift will simply pull the sleepers out of the ballast.

In the propped condition, the LNER's two 45-ton cranes were capable of lifting their maximum load from a minimum radius of 17ft out to 23ft. The carriages were mounted on a pair of two axle bogies producing axle loads of 20 tons and therefore clearly intended for use on lines constructed to heavy duty standards, rather than lightly-laid branches. The 33ft length of the jib, although longer than most earlier types, is still only regarded as being of medium length. The jib length of all subsequent breakdown cranes was to be greater still at 40 or more feet. The jib was supported while in train formation on a match truck of the well type (LNER wagon diagram 31). The purpose of the well was to make it easier for the breakdown crew to access the various items of heavy equipment carried on the wagon, such as spreader beams, lifting chains, shackles, timber packing, bridging rails etc.

As No ADM 1106 an ex-LNER 36-ton crane deals with an incident at Chinley on 23rd March 1979 in which a DMU was damaged in a collision. Note the propping girders drawn out from the carriage and blocked up on timbers to increase the crane's stability when making heavy lifts. The auxiliary hoist appears to have been removed. (M.S. Welch)

Atlantic

Pre-war 35/6-ton cranes

Having equipped itself with the means of handling its largest locomotives, the LNER was content for the time being to rely throughout the rest of the system on a varied selection of a couple of dozen generally short-jib steam breakdown cranes[2]. The capacity of these ranged from five at 35 tons down to eleven at 15 tons, together with a few 15 and 10-ton hand cranes. By the early 1930s, however, they appeared to have embarked on a policy of obtaining, finances permitting, one modern long-jibbed ever year or so. Certainly, Ransomes and Rapier of Ipswich supplied a 35-ton crane in 1932 (Order No. D4648), which was initially allocated to Cambridge and able to lift its maximum rated load at a radius of between 18 and 20ft. This and all subsequent cranes supplied to the company were provided with relieving bogies, in this case of the Stokes patent design. Relieving bogies are a pair of two axle bogies which, while in train formation, are structurally connected, one at either end of the carriage, but can be detached at the site operations, thereby enabling the crane to approach closer to the load to be lifted. The means of attachment permits rotation about the vertical access while rounding curves, but transmits a share of the crane's vertical load to each of the bogies. By this means the maximum axle load can be kept much lower and thereby affords the crane wide route availability.

In 1936 a further crane with relieving bogies was acquired, this time in the form of a crane from Cowans Sheldon capable of lifting when propped 36 tons at a radius of 18 to 25 ft (Works No. 5755)[1]. Its 40ft jib enabled it to reach out to a radius of 40ft on the main hoist when, as the table on the drawing, shows it could lift 18 tons, or 4½ tons when 'free on the rail'. In addition, it was equipped with a 6-ton auxiliary hoist for lighter work, the benefit being that it was faster in operation. This crane was paired with a purpose-built well-type match wagon similar to that provided four years earlier for the 35-ton Ransomes & Rapier crane for Cambridge. It

The relieving bogie to RS1106/36 with upturned emergency trolley on top. A screw jack within the bogie acting through the triangulated connection between the bogie and crane carriage was the means by which load was transferred from the crane to the bogie to even out the axle loads to an acceptable value while travelling in train formation. (P. Tatlow No. 35/95-21)

spent the first twenty years of its life stationed at Colwick, near Nottingham. Subsequently it was reassigned to the London Midland Region and was allocated to Toton in February 1967 and later Newton Heath until withdrawn. After 50 years' main line service it was acquired by Peak Rail at Buxton in December 1987.

Colwick's crane was followed a year later by a 35-ton crane from Cowans Sheldon (Works No. 6080) without the auxiliary hoist for Tweedmouth. The one ton reduction in maximum capacity appears to be entirely cosmetic to suit the specification of the North Eastern Area, which adopted this rather than 36 tons, and the design of the crane seems to be otherwise similar. The match wagon for this crane, on the other hand, was of a simpler design without a well

and no doubt cheaper but was equipped with automatic vacuum brake (LNER wagon diagram 136). Its arrival at Tweedmouth allowed an ex-NER 15-ton Cowans Sheldon crane of 1893 to be withdrawn. By the mid '60s the 35-ton crane had been transferred to Thornaby and was at York by 1970, before being withdrawn two years later and subsequently cut up.

Wartime 45-ton cranes

The rapidly deteriorating political situation in Europe during the latter part of the 1930s led the Government and the railway companies to consider the consequences and hence the precautions to be taken against aerial bombardment of our cities, industries and transport infrastructure. On land this last still largely meant the railways and various measures were put in hand to prepare for such an onslaught.

Ex-WD 45-ton oil-fired crane No. RS1085/45 in yellow livery is depicted on 5th January 1969 lowering a large metal girder from Bridge No. 138 Windsor Street, Salford, on the LNWR Liverpool-Manchester line. A man on his hands and knees is positioned on the right-hand side to give warning to the crane supervisor of any tendency for the rear wheels to lift off the rails. (M.S. Welch)

A pair of LNER Cowans Sheldon long-jib steam breakdown cranes is seen at work on the renewal of the superstructure to Bridge No. 6, Dunston Bridge, Newcastle on 25th November 1945. On the far bank is 35-ton No. 901630 from Tweedmouth assisted on the near side by 45-ton No. 901719 from Darlington. As well as the extended propping girders, note the steam turbine generator mounted on the cab sides to provide electricity for lighting.
(P. Tatlow collection)

These included the provision at Government expense of twelve 45-ton steam breakdown cranes for three of the companies, of which the LNER's share was six 45-ton cranes from the Cowans Sheldon stable again. The Great Western and Southern railways received four and two 45 ton cranes respectively from Ransomes and Rapier, while for the time being the LMS made do with five existing 36 ton cranes recently strengthened and uprated to 50-ton capacity[3].

It will be noticed that the previous two cranes could lift 36 tons to a radius of 25ft when propped, whilst the minimum radius was 18ft. By recognising that at reduced radius the stability of the crane permitted the lifting of even greater loads, the capacity of these cranes was increased to a maximum of 45 tons at 20ft radius. For this purpose, the strength of the hoisting tackle and winding gear was enhanced and the auxiliary hoist dispensed with. Otherwise the design was much as before, although the height of the relieving bogies was reduced and hydraulic jacks used instead of screw jacks to transfer the load from the crane to the bogie in running condition.

The length of the jib appears to have been increased by one foot. The match wagons were similar to these provided for the 35-ton crane of 1937, although the jib rest was repositioned and through vacuum brake pipe only was provided (LNER wagon diagram 160).

Delivery of these six cranes from Cowans Sheldon is believed to have started in late 1939 with Works No. 6870 for Thornton, followed in the New Year by the rest for New England, Darlington, Cambridge, Gorton and King's Cross. As a consequence of their arrival, existing cranes were released to be cascaded to other less strategic depots. In turn, other smaller cranes were reallocated, sometimes to depots previously without steam cranes. An example is that the above-mentioned Rapier 35-ton at Cambridge was moved to Stratford, releasing a medium-length jib ex-GER 35-ton Rapier crane of 1919 to be sent to Norwich Thorpe and its ex-GN 15 ton Cowans Sheldon of 1899 to Colchester.

Call to arms

Matters were not to be left undisturbed for long, however, as by 14th January 1942 Sir Alan Mount was reporting to the Railway Executive Committee that the Ministry of Supply on behalf of the War Office required six breakdown cranes of 35/45-ton capacity, two for urgent shipment to Iraq. Two days later the LNER offered to release the 45-ton cranes from Gorton and King's Cross. The Committee recommended that the remaining four be obtained from crane manufacturers. Replacements for the two cranes were requested. The LNER cranes were fitted with Westinghouse brake gear, converted to oil firing and given a lick of paint before being shipped to the Middle East. The two replacement cranes for the LNER were received from Ransomes and Rapier in 1943 (Order No. F4991/3) and duly took up duty at Gorton and King's Cross, enabling the temporary reversal of the cascading of 1940 to be finally implemented. In the meantime a member of the breakdown gang at Gorton, having been called up for military service, found himself put in charge of his own crane, now WD 210 stationed at Tehran, Persia (now Iran). Vigorous use of scouring

Eastfield's 45-ton crane attends to an overturned class K2 2-6-0, probably on the West Highland line as the encampment suggests the naval facilities beside Loch Long. Subsequently the 36-ton crane from St. Margaret's had to be brought in to assist restoring the engine on to the track.
(G.H.K. Lund collection, courtesy P. Lund)

Atlantic

powder soon revealed its original identity LNER, LOCO RUNNING DEPT, GORTON, 951515 between Arab script and its new WD No. These two cranes never returned to the United Kingdom and are believed to have remained in the Middle East.

On 12th October 1942, the MoS placed an order with Cowans Sheldon for eight 45-ton cranes (Works Nos. 8052 to 8059) and six from Ransomes and Rapier (Order No. F5937-49). Apart from a reversion to the earlier deeper design of relieving bogies, but still operated by hydraulic jacks, and oil-fired boilers, these were the same as the LNER's 45-ton cranes. They were delivered in 1943 and most found their way to Europe in 1944. One of the former, however, was sold as surplus to the Chief Civil Engineer's Department of the London Midland Region of British Railways in June 1960. This was put to work on bridge works as part of the implementation of the electrification of the West Coast Main Line under the Modernisation Plan and remained oil-fired for the time being. It was based at Basford Hall, Crewe, until taken on by the CME&E in November 1969 as regional spare at Bescot. As an Engineer's crane it was painted yellow long before this became the norm for breakdown cranes. We shall hear of this crane again later.

British Railways era

With the war over, the railways were attempting to restore their infrastructure, facilities and services against the increasing likelihood of nationalisation. As part of this process, the LNER placed an order with Cowans Sheldon for a further 36-ton crane with 6-ton auxiliary hoist. Delivery was not achieved until 1948 (Works No. 9017) when it was allocated to Immingham. It was generally similar to the Colwick crane, but there are minor differences resulting from experience over the intervening years. In 1972, this crane had its capacity uprated to 45 tons.

One notable development, however, was the adoption of an articulated jib foot. On all the cranes described so far the crane superstructure and jib had to be considered as a rigid body in plan when travelling round curves. The superstructure is able to rotate about the kingpin with the jib restrained by the jib rest on the match wagon, together with some restraint to the tail of the crane relative to the carriage. As a result, the radius of line curvature for the long-jibbed cranes, introduced during the period under review, was restricted. When lowered on to the match wagon the articulated jib on the other hand allowed some rotation at the jib foot and with the superstructure now locked relative to the carriage, the ability to negotiate curves was improved. The foot of the jib was made in the form of a crutch which, when horizontal, allowed the jib to be drawn forward and subsequently permit some movement between the jib and the crab sides. The match wagon jib support had a pair of inclined faces, which engaged with pins projecting from the jib sides, so that as the jib was lowered through the last stages the jib was drawn away from the crane. The match wagon was otherwise similar to those paired with the 45-ton cranes, although full vacuum brake equipment was restored (BR wagon diagram 630).

In 1968, following its transfer from Peterborough to March, No. 330110 (formerly 941599) suffered a buckling failure of the jib while making a heavy lift. As a result, its jib was replaced by an all-welded one with an articulated foot, similar to those fitted to the 75 and 30-ton cranes supplied to BR between 1959 and 1964. Details of the cranes and match wagons with numbers, allocations and eventual fate will be found in the attached Table. Like many breakdown cranes, it will be noted that all survived the demise of steam traction on British Railways in 1968 by a number of years. The former Tweedmouth crane was the first to succumb in September 1972, while the two 36 tonners with auxiliary hoist continued until the mid-1980s, both going into preservation following withdrawal.

Conversion to diesel propulsion

With the decline of the loose-coupled small goods wagon, prone to derail at the least provocation, the continuing need for a large fleet of breakdown cranes was unnecessary. The introduction of diesel locomotives called for cranes with the ability to lift their maximum load at greater outreach than previously required for more robustly-constructed steam engines and most cranes of less than 35-ton capacity had

The vertical boiler of RS1106/36 undergoing maintenance during which the manhole covers have been removed to reveal the cross tubes. Note the safety valves on the left, the folded-down chimney extension and flood lights on the corner of each counterweight.

(P. Tatlow No 35/95 -14)

left the scene by the end of the 1970s. Six new telescopic jib 75-tonne diesel-hydraulic cranes had been delivered by NEI/Cowans Sheldon in 1977/8, following which the ten former steam 75-ton cranes of 1961/2 had been converted to diesel propulsion to provide breakdown cranage into the future. Then in the mid-1980s, somewhat surprisingly, the four remaining ex-LNER 45-ton Cowans Sheldon cranes, together with the ex-WD acquired by the LM Region, were also selected for conversion. As with the 75-ton cranes, the work was carried out in the Crane Shop at Derby Locomotive Works. This involved removing the boilers, water tanks, coal boxes and cylinders and in their place providing a diesel engine to power hydraulic

Ex-LNER 36-ton Cowans Sheldon steam breakdown crane, formerly No. 941591, at Toton on 8th November 1969 following its transfer to the London Midland Region the year previous and renumbered as RS1106/36. Note the low floor level of the match wagon to ease the task of loading and offloading heavy items of lifting gear and packing timbers.

(P. Tatlow No. 35/95-29)

No. ADRC 96719, following withdrawal and sale to Phillips in April 1997 for scrapping, stands on a siding opposite the former Pullman Works at Preston Park, Brighton, in the summer of 1998. This crane was No. 941599 and has the replacement all welded articulated jib. (P. Tatlow No. 35/340/18A)

motors driving the original drive shaft. Additional ballast weights were fitted and the capacity enhanced to 50 tonnes at 6 metres (19.7 feet) radius. Their lives were not, however, markedly extended and withdrawals began within seven years. One has been preserved on the Llangollen Railway, while at the time of writing (June 1999) another still awaits scrapping.

Liveries

The livery worn by the pre-war cranes is unknown. It seems to me unlikely that they were painted Oxford blue, as applied to Engineer's vehicles, but I await readers' comments. It is more certain that the 45-tonners supplied at the beginning of the World War II were black with red lining and lettering in white or straw. The maker's name was applied along the jib sides in large cut-out aluminium letters. The first decade of nationalisation saw black continued with straw lettering, while clutch wheels and the back-ground to notice plates were red. A radical change in appearance took place following the issue of instructions in July 1959 that breakdown cranes were to be painted bright red with white lettering. The instructions allowed for black and straw lining, but I have no evidence that this was applied to an ex-LNER crane and the practice ceased from 1965. At the same time, the first stirring of safety considerations began to appear with the painting of jib heads white and the application of warning notices and ever increasing amounts of yellow and black diagonal hazard stripes. For those cranes repainted after 1977, which apart from the diesel conversions may have been few if any, an all-over unlined yellow livery with black lettering was applied.

Hornby-Dublo

Readers may recall that Hornby-Dublo introduced a red coloured die-cast metal steam breakdown crane in 1960. The die-cast process permitted some fine detail, but compromise was necessary in the matter of the winding handles, propping girders and over-length relieving bogies. It was stated at the time that this was based on a Cowans Sheldon 45-ton crane from the Eastern Region of British Railways. This challenged me to find out more about it and incidentally launched me into research of breakdown cranes. About two years later, I concluded that Hornby's model was a hybrid[4]. Its No. 133 is Cambridge's 45-tonner of 1940, but the jib is too short. I suspect that the 1940 example was originally intended, but the long jib led to difficulties in negotiating 15in radius curves and the solution was to substitute a shorter jib, probably from the 1926 version, and match wagon on a standard 17ft 6in underframe.

References:

1. *Locomotive Magazine*, p23, 15th February 1943.
2. Peter Tatlow, *LNER Wagons*, p176, Oxford Publishing Co 1976, or Pendragon 1998.
3. Peter Tatlow, *LMS breakdown arrangements*, pp 43-48, *British Railway Journal*, LMS Special Edition, 1988.
4. Peter Tatlow, '*Work at night*,' pp280-281, *Railway Modeller*, Vol. 11, (Dec) 1960.

Peterborough's 45-ton crane No. 941599 in black livery on 26th August 1952. This was kept near Peterborough North station to be ready for prompt action when required. The chimney is raised and the head of the driver can just be seen to the left of the pulley block attending to the machinery. (A.E. West, courtesy M.S. King R1668)

COWANS SHELDON 35/6 & 45 TON STEAM BREAKDOWN CRANES

LNER 38 scheme	1st BR/WD	2nd BR ADRC	Year built	Makers works/ Order No.	Max Cap (ton)	Match wagon No.	Remarks and Allocation	See Notes	Wthn	Disposal
941591	124	95223	1936	5755	36	941753	Colwick c'37 to 15/1/67, to LMR '68 No RS1106/36, Toton 2/67 to 10/85, Newton Heath.	1	c'87	Sold to Peak Rail ex Toton 12/87, Matlock 12/89
901630	(331)158	-	1937	6080	35	901715 2111	No 5, Tweedmouth 1/10/37 to 10/60, Thornaby '64 to 11/67, York 2/70.	-	9/72	
971588	RS1058/45	95220 96717	1939	6870	45	971589	Thornton Jct 1/40, Eastfield 10/42 to 10/83, Derby LW 10/84 to 10/85, Motherwell 4/88 to 2/91, Electrification Dept.	2	12/93	Scrapped at Ashford by Coopers Metals
941599	(330)110	95218 96719	1940	6871	45	941776	New England 2/40 to 2/68, March 2/68 to 1/79, Healey Mills 9/80, Derby LW 10/84 to 10/85, Brighton 4/88 to 2/91, Brighton (national spare) 9/94, Brighton OOU to 6/99. Replacement all welded articulated jib following accident c'68.	2	'96/'97	Sold to Phillips 4/97 for scrapping
901719	(331)156	95217 96716	1940	6872	45	901720	Darlington 6/40 to '64, Thornaby 2/68 to 9/80, Derby LW 10/84 to 10/85, Ashford Crane Repair Depot 4/88 to 2/91. Match wagon retained and converted into tunnel ventilation fan	2 10/85	12/93	Scrapped at Ashford by Coopers Metals
961606	(330)133	95219 96720	1940	6873	45	961665	Cambridge 6/40 to 4/72, Stratford 1/79, Inverness 9/80, Derby LW 10/84 to 10/85, Chart Leacon 4/88, Stewarts Lane (SR relief crane) 2/91, Electrification Dept Paddock Wood.	2 1/87	7/94	Scrapped at Ashford by Coopers Metals
951515	-	-	1940	6874	45	951675	Gorton 6/40, No WD 210	-	c'42	To WD, Tehran, Persia
941600	-	-	1940	6875	45	941766	King's Cross '40.	-	'42	To WD, for service in the Middle East
-	RS1085/45	95221 96718	1943	8053	45	DB 998523	Oil fired, Purchased from WD 6/60, to CCE Dept, Basford Hall, Crewe '62, to CMEE Dept Bescot as LM regional spare 11/11/69, Derby LW 10/84 to 10/85, Laira 4/88 to 3/95.	2 5/86	c'97	To Llangollen Rly 30/3/97
941602	966103	95222	1948	9017	36	DB 998500	Immingham '48, Grimsby, Finsbury Park 8/78, Thornaby, Up-rated to 45T capacity '72, Derby Loco Wks.	1	Yes	Dean Forest Rly, Norchard 4/4/86 to 11/8/95, GCR, Ruddington 4/96 to 26/8/96

Notes:

1. 6 ton auxiliary hoist
2. Converted to diesel hydraulic
3. Dates shown in italics are spot dates upon which the crane is known to have been at the depot concerned

The LNER's post-war order for a 36-ton crane with 6-ton auxiliary hoist was only fulfilled by Cowans Sheldon after nationalisation. Here No. DB 966103 is rerailing an errant Class 08 diesel shunter at West Street Junction, Boston, in 1969.

(N.H. Pigott /32A)

TPO Service on the LN

King's Cross
- Leeds

ER

An early LNER view at Ganwick c.1924 shows A1 No. 1476 of King's Cross (later named Royal Lancer) with the up train and one of the ex-GNR clerestory TPOs. Behind the tender is an ex-GNR double-door milk van, a batch of which was converted to stowage vans soon after construction. The passenger accommodation is moderate with a mixture of gangwayed and six-wheel carriages.

(Roger Carpenter Collection)

A1 No. 4471 Sir Frederick Banbury, *another Doncaster locomotive still with short lap valves, leaves Wood Green Tunnel c.1929-30 with a similar formation. It's clear that photographers knew all about this train and this is one of the better efforts to frame the loco and TPO.*

(Author's Collection)

BY STEVE BANKS

When the memorable film 'The Night Mail' was produced by the LMS and the General Post Office in the 1930s Travelling Post Offices gained something of an aura that they have never lost. The film described the dedicated postal service between Euston and the far north. Operating practices on the LNER differed because this company's TPOs were attached in ones, twos and threes to a variety of expresses which conveyed passengers and appeared in the public timetable. There were three streams: King's Cross to Newcastle /Edinburgh, King's Cross to Leeds and the East Anglian service from Liverpool Street. These notes focus on how the service to Leeds was worked by the LNER (Great Northern Section) during which several phases can be identified.

The Great Northern Railway had a long history of postal services and in the first years of the twentieth century was operating three main ones as far north as Newcastle, the precursor of the Leeds service being the 'Great Northern Sorting Carriage' which ran King's Cross-Doncaster-Leeds, empty to York, then York-King's Cross the following day. When some of the services between King's Cross, Newcastle and Edinburgh were amalgamated on 10th July 1922 a separate King's Cross-Leeds TPO was instigated. It ran for nearly twenty years until 21st September 1940 when the wartime Blitz over London was beginning to intensify. Initially called the 'Leeds Sorting Carriage', the service was later known, internally at least, as the 'Doncaster-London TPO' when those were the points between which Post Office staff were employed to do sorting.

The mail vans

The LNER inherited about a dozen bogie TPOs at the grouping and no new ones were built for six years. The ex-GNR vehicles comprised two old clerestory-roofed types with bow ends (GN.316) and three that Gresley had built to his classic outline (GN.313 and GN.312):

Built	Diagram	GN No.	LNER No.
1902	GN.316	1043	4204
1902	"	1045	4205
1907	GN.313	1858	4202
1909	"	2407	4203
1913	GN.312	1969	4201

The earliest diagram was to a length of 51ft 6in while the two by Gresley, which only differed in detail, were 56ft 6in long. Traductor gear and nets were fitted on both sides. (Nos. 4202-3 were deployed on the King's Cross-Newcastle-Edinburgh service. In 1933 they were sent to the Great Eastern Section and renumbered 6133-4).

For the Leeds service three TPOs were required. Details of the workings follow and it suffices here to say that, as far as can be ascertained, during the first period after the grouping No. 4201 worked daily with one of the other two vehicles, the clerestory-roofed pair Nos. 4204-5, which alternated. In reserve was one of the ex-GNR close-coupled six-wheel pairs Nos. 4206+4207. In an emergency one of the alternating clerestory TPOs could have been pushed into working out and back the same day but time for such a manoeuvre would have been short. The accompanying photograph which shows one of the clerestory TPOs in the afternoon up working may have arisen through pooling of the three bogie vehicles or as a switch after the unavailability of No. 4201 and a desire not to use the six-wheel reserve.

In December 1932 and June 1933, when more LNER-built TPOs were being delivered to the North Eastern Area for the King's Cross-

One of the ex-NER mailvans that was transferred to the Leeds service in 1932 and renumbered 4208, seen here at an LNER exhibition.
(D. Williamson Collection)

Newcastle-Edinburgh service, two ex-NER TPOs were cascaded to the GN Section:

Built	Diagram	NEA No.	GN Section No.
1904	NE.93	2292	4208
"	"	2295	4209

These were 52ft clerestories, similar in length to the ex-GNR clerestories but with exchange gear on one side only which gave them a greater capacity for sorting. They took over from the older clerestories alternating opposite No. 4201, the ousted vehicles going into reserve. This phase lasted about four years until brand-new LNER-built TPOs were at last provided for the Leeds service.

Construction of LNER-designed TPOs had actually begun in 1929 to D.131 when three were provided for the NE Area, allowing a similar number of ex-NER vehicles to be transferred to the GE Section. Replacement of an increasingly aged fleet gathered pace in the period between 1933-37 when fourteen more TPOs were built to D.164 and D.165. Here is a complete listing which shows the company's priorities at the time. As can be seen, ten more new vans were allocated to the NE Area where the mileages were greatest ('2XXX' numbers), their arrival allowing the previous trio to D.131 to be transferred to the GE Section ('6XXX' numbers). The Leeds service had to soldier on until 1936-7 when four new mail vans were at last supplied ('4XXX' numbers). It was the last of the LNER postal services to be modernised.

1929	D.131	2260.86.2339	(3)
		(6130-2 in 1933)	
1933	D.165	2151-4	(4)
"	D.164	2155-7	(3)
1936	"	4202-3	(2)
1937	"	4206-7	(2)
"	"	2440-2	(3)

The four new mail vans for the GN Section allowed three to work daily with the fourth in reserve. Their arrival finally displaced all the pre-group TPOs on the Leeds service, the ex-GNR clerestories having served for over a third of a century. From 1937 all the TPOs in the Leeds service were LNER standard designs and completely interchangeable.

Differences between the three LNER dia-grams were relatively small, especially D.164/5 which only varied in detail. All were built on the standard 60ft underframe with plain ends and traductor gear and nets on one side only. This gave substantially more room for sorting racks but also meant that vehicles which exchanged bags in both directions had to be turned, though in practice nearly all the exchanges during the late 1930s on the Leeds service were made in the same direction. After various gangway positions in the earlier vans, both central and offset, the British Standard design was fitted in the offset position, away from the sorting racks, again allowing maximum use of the interior.

The service

The following notes describe the formations of the trains and how they were worked. It is convenient to begin with the down service which during the 1930s left King's Cross just after dawn at 4.45am. Containing two main portions for the West Riding and the North East, it comprised a mixture of parcels and mail-vans (to quote LNER terminology) with the odd carriage for passengers to all the principal points. No opportunity to convey passengers was missed with a departure from King's Cross, even at this early an hour! By the summer of 1939 it was a heavy train which in midweek was made up to fourteen vehicles as follows. For the sake of clarity I have used the standard abbreviations where 'K' indicated gangwayed

passenger, 'B' indicates brake, 'C' indicates composite and 'T' indicates third. 'L' (only used with non-corridor coaches) indicates lavatory. For the vans I have distinguished between gangwayed and non-gangwayed vans by using BG and BV respectively.

4.45am ex-King's Cross	
CK	York
TK	"
BG	Newcastle
BG	Darlington
BV	York
BG	Edinburgh
BV	Leeds
BV	"
CK	"
TPO	"
TPO	"
BCK	Bradford
BV	Grimsby
BV	Peterborough

Four-wheeled vehicles could also be attached "when necessary from London upon authority from Office of Superintendent".

Each of the main portions included a couple of passenger carriages, the West Riding portion carrying one each for Leeds and Bradford. Being a GN Main Line service, the GN Section was responsible for the stock and most came from its pool. The exception was the clutch of BGs with the most northerly destinations. These three vans were part of the

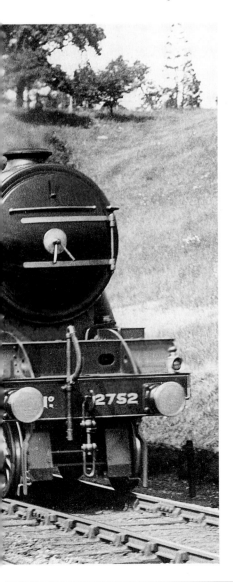

E470E at Hornsey in 1958, one of the ex-GNR milk vans of 1920 to GN.309 as converted to a Stowage Van with offset BS gangways. Almost 40 years later it is still in service, now coupled to an ex-LNER TPO.
(D.C. Seabrook)

ECS fleet and consisted of LNER-built vans of the mid-1920s: two to D.43 (teak) and one to D.45 (all-steel). The latter, the premier vehicle, was used for the Scottish service.

The rest of the train was provided by the GN Section. The TPOs by now were LNER standards, as was the brake composite to Bradford which was a recently-built example to D.175 and pretty well the most common type. Everything else - almost two-thirds of the train - was of GNR origin, the vans in this train (and the others in the Leeds TPO service) being drawn from the pool of Howlden 45ft flat-roof vans to GN.296, Gresley elliptical-roof 51ft 1½in to GN.293/307 which were fairly similar ordinary vans and GN.309/310 which were the milk version with four sets of double doors on either side that made them eminently suitable for the rapid transfer of mailbags at the various stops (viz. the two BVs in the Leeds portion). It was common for overnight trains out of the public eye to deploy older vans and this train was no exception, hence the unusually high pre-group content still in the train in 1939. In this aspect relatively little had changed since the grouping.

Graded as an Express Passenger and probably behind one of King's Cross's Pacifics, the train ran non-stop to Peterborough. The TPOs were busy at six places, however, with exchange of mailbags near Langley, Hitchin, Biggleswade and St. Neots and delivery near Sandy and Huntingdon North. At Peterborough the two vans at the rear were dropped off.

There was no further use of the exchange gear north of Peterborough and stops were made at all the principal stations. In fact, stops were also made at Essendine and in the section between Retford and Doncaster at Ranskill, Bawtry and Rossington. Long-distance passengers would doubtless have queried the train's status as an express in the last ten miles before Doncaster when the train was effectively serving as an early morning local passenger.

On reaching Doncaster at 8.21am the two main portions were divided and strengthened with more passenger carriages for what was probably a regular trip for a modest number of commuters north of Doncaster. With its widespread conurbation, the West Riding was something of a backwater compared with the East Coast Main Line but a busy one. Hence a great deal of old stock was employed in its many shuttle services, much of it as articulated sets of former six-wheel carriages so it is not surprising that one of them was attached for the trip to Leeds.

Rather more unusual for the ECML in this late a period - the last normal timetable before the outbreak of World War II - was the strengthening of the portion to York with two vintage ex-GNR six-wheel carriages. It was still a GN Section train, of course, and it came away first:

8.28am ex-Doncaster	
BT (6w)	York
C (6w)	"
CK	"
TK	"
BG	Newcastle
BG	Darlington
BV	York
BG	Edinburgh

Now made up with an equal mixture of vans and passenger carriages, the train reached York at 9.18am where it was divided again with the three principal vans attached to further northbound trains. The BG at the rear received the highest priority because it was designated "To convey Letter Mails, Urgent News, Luggage and Parcels for Newcastle and North thereof and Parcel Post for destinations north of Edinburgh". Within twenty minutes of arrival it had been transferred by the station pilot to the 9.38am York-Edinburgh express and was on its way.

Recently built A3 No. 2752 Spion Kop *(DON) leaves Hadley Wood Tunnel in June 1929 with No. 4201 and a pair of ex-GNR non-corridor twins.*
(Author's Collection).

A rare view of the whole train c.1930 with A1 No. 4473 Solario *(DON) in charge. Trailing the TPO and ex-GNR twins are five Howlden and Gresley bogie vans.*
(Author's Collection)

The second train had departed Doncaster a mere five minutes after the York portion:

8.33am ex-Doncaster

BT-C-BT*	Leeds
BV	"
BV	"
CK	"
TPO	"
TPO	"
BCK	Bradford

*Articulated triplet of ex-GNR six-wheel carriages

The train reached Leeds at 9.20am having stopped only twice en route, at Wakefield to detach the Bradford carriage and at Holbeck (later called Holbeck High Level) on the outskirts of Leeds where travellers into town would have been picked up. Holbeck in those days was a busy station and good reason for stopping what locals were likely to have called 'the morning mail train'.

The up workings were a different kettle of fish because the two mailvans were divided at Leeds and sent back to London by separate trains at markedly different times of the day. In 1939 the first departure was at midday, 12.02pm to be precise, when one of the TPOs was conveyed to Doncaster by a local, all-stations service. It was detached and held there until 4.56pm when it left with three non-corridor passenger carriages and, at the rear, six bogie vans, one from Doncaster, the rest from Hull and Grimsby Town. On Saturdays a four-wheel 'red van' from Nottingham (probably carrying tobacco traffic from the Player's factory) was picked up along the way and detached at Peterborough. Though graded as an express and rostered for one of Doncaster's Pacifics,

this was more of a semi-fast working with numerous stops along the way and King's Cross wasn't reached until 9.13pm.

During the early 1930s the timing was similar although fewer vans were conveyed while the passenger accommodation, as befits a train of modest status at a time of change, was more variable. Here are the midweek listings for two years in sufficient detail to show the nature of the stock and the leisurely pace of modernisation in such services:

4.56 Doncaster-King's Cross

Summer	1934
TPO	ex-GNR GN.312
CL	Howlden GN.129
T	ex-NER
T	ex-NER
BCL	Howlden GN.189
BV	Gresley GN.307
BV	Gresley GN.310
Summer	1939
TPO	LNER
CL	Howlden GN.129
BT-CL	LNER 55ft 6in twin
BV	Gresley GN.307
BV	Howlden GN.296
BV	Gresley GN.307
BV	Gresley GN.310
BV	Gresley GN.293
BV	Gresley GN.293

The formation of 1934 was entirely pre-group with a pair of recently-cascaded coaches from the NE Area, an early attempt to replace ancient stock from the turn of the century with something at least a little newer. When the train was observed by the late R.G.C. Stephenson leaving Doncaster on New Year's Eve 1934 with No. 2543 *Melton* in charge, behind the mail van were four ex-GNR

coaches, an equal mixture of non-corridor and gangwayed and a Howlden brake van. On another occasion four fish vans from Hull or Grimsby had been added. Confounded by the mixture, Ray Stephenson described the train as a "slow" despite the express lights that would undoubtedly have been carried.

The Howlden 45ft lavatory composite with only 30 seats was still running in 1939, getting on for half a century older than and in striking contrast to the recently-built outer suburban Gresley twin alongside. The vans were still a mixture of Howlden and Gresley vans ex-GNR.

Few records have survived for the 1920s when the TPO is believed to have run attached to an express from Leeds to reach King's Cross much earlier (the times varied between 3.50pm and 4.40pm). This, however, was ideal for photographers near London and we have quite a few images from the period, many of them carefully composed by a tunnel where the locomotive and TPO could be framed together. At first, mixed sets of ex-GNR non-catering gangwayed and non-corridor stock were recorded, then non-corridor twins. The locomotives seen were a King's Cross Pacific c1924 but Doncaster ones later (all working south of Doncaster at a time before Pacifics were allowed as far as Leeds). As far as can be ascertained the mailvan's path was changed c1931 to reach King's Cross some four or five hours later as already described.

The second mailvan left Leeds long after

A1 2543 Melton *of Doncaster c.1927-29 with short lap valves leaves Hadley Wood Tunnel with ex-GNR TPO No. 4201 behind the tender. The lettering on the TPO is 'LNER 4201 Royal Mail'. The crests are placed mid-panel underneath. Beyond the TPO is another ex-GNR carriage, an eight-wheel clerestory composite.*
(Author's Collection)

darkness had fallen in the 10.23pm express to King's Cross. This was another overnight service with three passenger carriages and a raft of vans, some more from Bradford being added to the rear en route at Wakefield. Further addition was made at Doncaster, this time to the front end where three mailvans from the King's Cross-Newcastle-Edinburgh service were transferred from the 8.00pm ex-Newcastle. The imposing fourteen-coach formation with four TPOs at the head left Doncaster at 11.34pm as follows (Sunday nights and Monday mornings excepted with daily detail variations simplified for the sake of clarity):

TPO	ex-Newcastle
TPO	"
TPO	"
TPO	ex-Leeds
BV	"
CK	"
TK	"
BCK	"
BG	"
BG	"
BG	ex-Bradford
BV	"
BG	"
BV	"

E70291E, a Gresley TPO to D.164 at Bounds Green in Early BR days. These LNER-built vans weren't provided for the Leeds service until the late 1930s by which time the schedules had been changed and the up train reached London in the hours of darkness. (D.C Seabrook)

Of all the TPO workings on the LNER this train, by its combination of services south of Doncaster, was the heaviest in terms of postal vehicles. Yet apart from the TPOs it was another typical GN Section train with ex-GNR passenger carriages and vans, even in

the summer of 1939. All the BVs were of GNR origin, as was the 56ft 6in BG from Bradford. The other BGs were LNER-built standards. Most of the BGs appeared in this train as part of a complex return working which had seen them travel out the previous night attached to an ECML sleeping car express.

The BV adjacent to the Leeds TPO is of interest because it was designated 'For Mails'. Built in 1920 to GN.309, it was one of the milk versions with four sets of double doors and useful for stowing sacks of mail next to the TPO. (Stowage vans proper were fitted with gangways that gave direct access to the TPO and the GNR had built a pair to GN.314 but they are not known to have worked to Leeds. Some of the milk vans to GN.309 were converted to stowage vans and one source suggests pre-1923 but this and their deployment in LNER days await clarification).

Once away from Doncaster the formation was fixed and stops were only made at the principal stations and Finsbury Park. A single exchange of mailbags was made near Huntingdon North though it is not known if it was carried out by the Leeds TPO or from the Newcastle trio. If the latter then the Leeds TPO would not need to have been turned (at both Leeds and London) in order to present the exchange gear which, from 1936-7, was on only one side of the Leeds TPOs.

The train reached King's Cross at 3.45am, alas too early to be photographed by the many photographers resident there. (It is a pity that the more accessible daylight arrival of the down working at Leeds doesn't seem to have been recorded either). Exactly one hour later the down working set off at 4.45am with the mail van that had come in earlier and the TPO that alternated with the one just arrived, details as already described.

Thus was the daily cycle by which the LNER and the GPO served the route between London and Leeds.

Postscript
My thanks go to Messrs. C.S. Carter, J. Edgson, P. Holmes, R. Tarpey, D. Williamson, Dr. G. Hughes and the Gresley Society. I would like to have been able to say more about workings pre-1931 but an essential source, an LNER (GN Main Line) Carriage Working book for the period, has yet to be found. Any helpful information would be welcome via the Editor, please.

THE G.E.R. N7 0-

by Lyn D. Brooks

Locomotives Information Co-ordinator
Great Eastern Railway Society

The prototype GER Class L77 0-6-2T No.1000 on a typically murky day at Liverpool Street on 10th March 1915.
(LCGB Ken Nunn Collection 1931)

By the 1923 grouping, the Great Eastern Railway was operating the most intensive steam suburban train service ever seen in the world. It came to do so largely by accident, as a consequence of opening its new City terminus at Liverpool Street in 1874. The extension from the old and inconveniently-sited Eastern Counties Railway terminus at Bishopsgate was coupled with a new line through north east London. This was built primarily to enable trains between London and the Cambridge main line to bypass the busy junction at Stratford on the Colchester line. The new line branched away northwards at Bethnal Green and passed through Hackney Downs and Clapton before joining the Cambridge line to the south of Tottenham. An extension of this new line continued north eastwards across the Lea Valley to Walthamstow and ultimately to Chingford.

Parliamentary sanction for the GER's 'Metropolitan Extensions' was gained on condition that the railway offered cheap workmen's fares on all trains from the Chingford and Enfield lines that terminated at Liverpool Street before 8.00am. This philanthropic condition was intended to compensate the 2,000-odd families whose homes would have to be demolished to build the extensions, for they were expected to remove themselves to the suburbs and travel to work by train. The homes that were demolished were almost entirely slum dwellings and the slum dwellers merely moved locally to the other slums, such as those of Hoxton. Meanwhile, it was the higher-paid artisans and clerks who flocked to Enfield and Walthamstow to take advantage of the cheap fares. And take advantage they did; many of the GER's new-found passengers travelled up to town on the cheap fares and

whiled away an hour or so before having to start work. As a result, the population of Walthamstow - for example - increased ten-fold in twenty years.

By 1900 what should have been a gold mine for the Great Eastern Railway had rapidly become a millstone around its neck. The trains were as long as possible and ran as frequently as the signalling system would allow, but they were still hopelessly overcrowded. The railway received nothing but complaints about the services, but they barely covered their operating costs.

By 1900 the inner suburban services were mainly in the hands of the R24 class 'Buckjumper' 0-6-0Ts of 1890. These were a product of the GER's most famous Locomotive Superintendent, James Holden, and were a development of his T18 design for shunting of 1886. They were assisted by three classes of

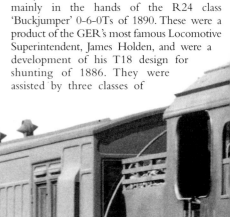

2 TANK ENGINES

No.69696 was originally LNER No.2656, one of the vacuum-only Beardmore-built N7/2s of 1927. It was rebuilt with a round-topped boiler in July 1946 and fitted with vacuum-operated push-pull gear in November 1951. Latterly class N7/5, it is seen here at Copley Hill shed on 3rd August 1956. Note the steel cab roof with sliding ventilator, with which all N7s were latterly fitted.

(A.G. Ellis, M&GN Railway Circle RSO 213)

Class N7/1 0-6-2T No.987 was one of the batch built in 1925-26 by Robert Stephenson & Co. Here it seems to be hauling an excursion train – probably to Southend – and typically composed of suburban stock. The carriages are former four-wheelers mounted on new bogie underframes.

(GERS Collection)

LEFT: *No.1003 of the second GER-built saturated L77s, completed in July 1921. Note the larger Westinghouse pump mounted adjacent to the smokebox. The engine is painted in the GER wartime grey livery, with the addition of the 1921 'Train Control' numerals painted on the side tanks.*
(Author's Collection)

CENTRE: *Gorton-built N7/5 No. 69630 enters Bethnal Green on 10th September 1960 with a Chingford train. This engine was unusual in having the BR smokebox door numberplate mounted lower down than on most engines, the door probably being second-hand from a scrapped D15/2 'Belpaire Claud' 4-4-0, with no destination board brackets.*
(G. Pember)

LOWER: *No.2607 was one of the first batch of ten N7/3s constructed at Doncaster Works, which were originally fitted with GN-pattern strapped smokebox doors. The N7/3s were similar to the N7/2s, but with round-topped fireboxes. The engine is seen here at Stratford shed in the early 1930s.*
(P. Ransome-Wallis)

0-4-4Ts to the designs of Holden's predecessors, S.W. Johnson, W. Adams and M. Bromley, all of which had been modernised under Holden, and a further 0-4-4T class of his own design. The outer suburban work was in the hands of the M15 class 2-4-2Ts of T.W. Worsdell's design and the larger C32 class derived from Holden's own mixed traffic 2-4-0s.

The 0-6-0Ts were rebuilt with higher-pressure boilers and larger tanks from 1902 and further new engines appeared based upon these rebuilds. The older 0-4-4Ts were coming due for replacement by this time, but no more of the Holden design were built and instead the old Worsdell 2-4-2T design was resurrected for further construction from 1903. Meanwhile, new express passenger engines and heavy goods 0-6-0s had appeared with more modern features, culminating in the S69 class '1500' 4-6-0s of 1911 with Belpaire boilers, superheaters and piston valves.

Thus by the period of the First World War the suburban services were being handled by locomotives that - although of modern construction - were still very much of Victorian design. However, matters were finally taken in hand under the direction of Alfred J. Hill, who had succeeded to the title of Locomotive Superintendent in 1912. In early 1914 orders were issued for producing the drawings for a new 0-6-2 tank engine, followed by order L77 for the construction of two locomotives to be numbered 1000 and 1001.

Apart from minor fittings, the engines were a totally new design. The driving wheels were 4ft 10in in diameter, driven by two inside cylinders of 18in diameter and 24in stroke. They were the first (and only) GER tank engines to have piston valves and of a generous 9½in diameter, whilst - unusually for an inside-cylinder locomotive - they were driven by Walschaerts motion. This was a wise choice, for with only two eccentrics mounted on the crank axle instead of four, there was plenty of room for generous big-end bearings, crank webs and axlebox journals.

The trailing carrying wheels had radial axleboxes and were of 3ft 9in diameter, whilst the leading coupled wheels had 'side traversing axleboxes', a GER speciality. These axleboxes were allowed a degree of sideplay, controlled by nests of coil springs let into the axlebox flanges, whilst the leading section of the coupling rods had a vertical hinge. To prevent the leading crankpin from binding, the bush had curved vertical faces to enable them to turn in the coupling rod ends.

The boilers were of 4ft 9in diameter, with a 9ft 7in barrel and a 6ft Belpaire firebox. To provide a comparison, No.1001 was fitted with a twelve element Robinson superheater, whilst No.1000 was a normal saturated engine. The superheated engine had twin GER-pattern snifting valves mounted behind the chimney to cool the superheater elements when coasting and No.1000 also had them to counteract the higher vacuum produced by the piston valves when running with steam off. Top-feed was supplied to the dome and the firebox was surmounted by the usual four column Ramsbottom safety valves used by the GER on 180lbs psi boilers. The nominal tractive effort was 20,512lbs and the engines had an adhesive weight of 49 tons 15 cwt.

The engines were built at Stratford and

Notes:

A. Nos. 8000, 8002-8011 saturated as built, superheated 1928-31

B. Nos. 8000-8012 renumbered 7978-7989, 1944

C. Works numbers calculated, not official

D. Rebuilds originally classified N7/3, reclassified N7/5 from 1952

E. Steam brake plus vacuum ejector as built. Two engines,
   2649/55 (69689/95) not rebuilt to N7/3

Class N7 0-6-2Ts: Building, Numbering and Rebuilding Details

LNER Numbers	Total	Builder	Date	Works Nos.	Class	Rebt. to	Date	1946 Numbers	Note
8000-8001	2	Stratford(L77)	1914-15	1569/72			1943-44	9600-9601	ABC
8002-8011	10	Stratford(K85)	1921	1623-32	N7/GE	N7/4	1940-49	9602-9611	ABC
7990-7999	10	Stratford(K89)	1923-24	1672/4-82			1940-48	9612-9621	BC
409/21/6/56/7 460/4/71/3/5 826-30/2-4/7/8 850-3/65-8 870/3	30	Gorton	1925-27	–			1943-56	9622-9651	D
907/12/3/6/8/9 935/40/1/7/50 952/64/6-8 970/1/87/8	20	R. Stephenson	1925-26	3897-916	N7/1	N7/5	1943-55	9652-9671	D
2632-2641	10	Gorton	1927-28	–	N7/2	N7/3	1943-52	9672-9681	
2642-2661	20	W. Beardmore	1927	305-24			1943-55	9682-9701	E
2600-2631	32	Doncaster	1927-28	1669-92 1696-9 1701/2/4/6	N7/3	–	–	9702-9733	

number 1000 was completed in December 1914, entering service two months later, still in 'photographic grey' livery. No.1001 was ex-works in January 1915 and it was handed over to the Running Department in March, the only engine of the type to carry the full GER blue livery. Externally, the engines had a powerful and imposing appearance, matched only perhaps by Ivatt's and Gresley's 0-6-2Ts for the Great Northern Railway - most other British locomotives of this wheel arrangement appeared longer and leaner. The boiler was pitched at 8ft 9in above rail level, the smokebox featuring the characteristic GER door with burnished steel ring in place of conventional hinge straps. This type of smokebox door was first introduced on the 'Claud Hamilton' 4-4-0s of 1900 and had been also used on the 4-4-0 rebuilds of the T19 2-4-0s when fitted with superheaters, as well as on the S69 '1500' 4-6-0s. The L77 0-6-2Ts were thus the only GER tank engines with this feature. The cabs were large, with high arched roofs and side windows, and the tanks appeared small by comparison, but nevertheless held 1,600 gallons of water.

The two engines were an immediate success; they could move the heavy suburban trains with ease, and whilst their larger driving wheels gave them greater speed than the 0-6-0Ts, their greater tractive effort enabled them to accelerate just as quickly. Wartime conditions meant that it was not possible to contemplate building further engines until 1921, when ten more were built to Letter Account K85, numbered 1002-1011. These engines had saturated boilers and some authors have opined that this was due to indecision as to whether No.1001's superheated boiler was worthwhile. However, the most likely reason was because of materials and manpower shortages following the Great War; contemporary batches of replacement boilers for the 'Claud Hamilton' 4-4-0s were also saturated, although superheaters had been standard on the class since 1913. There were also some other detail differences between the new engines and the prototypes principally in that the dome was moved further forward, the cab roof was of quasi-elliptical shape, and larger

8/8½in Westinghouse pumps were fitted. They were finished in the GER's wartime grey livery, which was continued up to - and well beyond - the grouping.

At the 1923 grouping the GER L77 class became LNER Class N7 and a further ten engines to Letter Account K89 were ordered in March. These entered service in 1923-4 as Nos.990E-999E and proved to be the last new engines built at Stratford. These differed from the foregoing in having superheaters, this time with eighteen elements, lower firebox crowns and other minor alterations. In line with LNER policy, they were fitted with vacuum ejectors, although the engine brakes remained Westinghouse. In common with other ex-GER locomotives, 7000 was later added to the pre-grouping numbers of the LNER, so that they occupied the LNER series 7990-8011. Of the ten 1924 engines, only Nos.998E and 999E went to Stratford depot initially and the first eight were distributed between Ardsley, Bradford and Hatfield. The Ardsley and Bradford locomotives had moved to Stratford by the close of 1924, but in May of the following year six of this batch of N7s were temporarily transferred to Neasden to work between Marylebone and Wembley in connection with the British Empire Exhibition of 1925. By the end of the year all ten were at work on the GE suburban services.

The LNER-built N7s

It is a great tribute to the GER design that Nigel Gresley, the Chief Mechanical Engineer of the new LNER, adopted the N7s as a standard design, in tandem with his own largely-similar N2s which he had produced for the Great Northern. 50 new N7s were ordered initially, 30 from the ex-GCR works at Gorton and twenty from Robert Stephenson & Co. Further changes were made to the design in line with the newly-adopted LNER standards and so the new N7s had 'flowerpot' chimneys, lower domes and an altered cab profile to bring them within the loading gauge of the Metropolitan 'Widened Lines' between King's Cross and Moorgate. Other alterations included singlering boilers with the feed to the backplate, 'pop' safety valves and left-hand drive. These engines were known as Class N7/1, the original machines becoming 'N7/GE'.

The N7/1s were delivered in 1925-27 and meanwhile another thirty were placed on order. Ten of these were built at Gorton and the remaining twenty by Beardmore & Co., delivered in 1927-28. They were classified N7/2, for they had long-travel gear and pony trucks in place of the radial axle, with smaller carrying wheels. In addition, the 'side traversing' leading axleboxes were replaced by the plain type and the bunker sides were raised. This eliminated the coal rails and the rear cab spectacles were circular. The cab side windows on the GER engines and the N7/1s were of the droplight type, but on the N7/2s they were moved closer to the doorway and were of the horizontally-sliding pattern. The twenty Beardmore locomotives were steam braked, with vacuum ejectors, whilst the ten Gorton engines were dual braked, as before.

The final 32 locomotives were all built by Doncaster Works in 1927-28 and these differed in having round-top firebox boilers, being classified N7/3. The first ten to be built had GNR-type strapped smokebox doors, but the remainder had the standard GE ringed pattern, as did all engines latterly. The accompanying table shows the building and numbering details of all of the N7 variants.

Many of the LNER-built locomotives were initially run in at depots close to their places of building, such as at Ardsley, Gorton and Eastfield, but by 1931 all had gravitated to the London area. The vacuum-braked N7/2s Nos. 2642-2661 settled down on the ex-GN section, with the remaining Westinghouse engines on the GE lines where they displaced the 0-6-0Ts from suburban work. At this time, a number of GNR-design N2 0-6-2Ts also worked on the GE section. However, experience showed that the larger driving wheels of the N2s were better-suited to the

Class N7/1 0-6-2T No.826 at the head of an up suburban train on the Colchester main line, shortly after building by Gorton Works in 1926.

(Author's Collection)

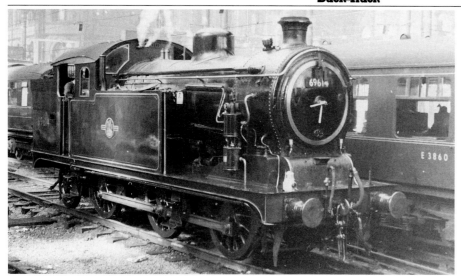

LEFT: *No.69614 was selected to act as West Side pilot at Liverpool Street in the 1950s, where it is seen in the summer of 1960 in typically immaculate condition. Originally No.992E, it was rebuilt as an N7/4 with round-topped boiler in February 1940 and was withdrawn in December 1960.*
(L. Ward)

CENTRE: *No.990E was the first of the final batch of GER-design engines, seen here ex-works in December 1923 in early LNER livery. These engines were superheated and had vacuum ejectors from the start.*
(GERS Collection 798.2535)

LOWER: *Following the reversion to regular manning of the N7s in the mid-1950s the crews applied special embellishments to the engines, such as the white-painted smokebox door ring sported by N7/5 No. 69668. Here it is seen at Stamford Hill with an Enfield Town train in May 1960. The overhead wires are already in position for the electrification of these services, which was inaugurated in the following November.*
(T. Wright 3140)

Westinghouse braked. In consequence the original twelve ex-GE N7s 8000-8011 were never fitted with vacuum ejectors and remained 'single-pipers' until the end.

The LNER-built engines were also modified in a similar manner to the GER locomotives. The N7/1s were fitted with additional coal rails and the cab roofs of all varieties were replaced by steel ones. The bunkers of all N7s – including the ex-GER examples – were fitted with either one or two footsteps in the sides, of various patterns. Ten new Belpaire boilers were built from 1930 for reboilering the N7/1s and N7/2s and as these were also intended for use on the ex-GE engines they had provision for top feed to the domes, having blanking plates on their sides. However, they were only ever used on the LNER locomotives and after top feed was abandoned, plain dome covers were eventually fitted. All the N7s had been built with condensing gear, but this was removed from them all in 1935-1938.

By 1940 further new boilers were required for the original GER engines and it was decided to fit them with the round-topped variety as used on the N7/3s. Thus all 22 engines were rebuilt down to 1949 and they were reclassified N7/5. In a similar way, the Belpaire-boilered N7/1s and N7/2s were fitted with round-topped boilers from 1943. At first, these rebuilds were included in Class N7/3, but as the ex-N7/1 rebuilds had short-travel valve gear, they were given the classification N7/5 from 1952. All 50 N7/1s thus became N7/5 by 1956, but not all the N7/2s were rebuilt, for withdrawal commenced in 1957.

The locomotives inherited by the LNER in 1923 had been renumbered by the simple addition of several thousand to their pre-grouping numbers. Thus ex-NER engines retained their original numbers, ex-GNR engines were increased by 3000, those from the GCR by 5000 and so on. New locomotives were given blank numbers, or those vacated by engines that had been scrapped. Twenty years later, the number of pre-grouping locomotives in stock had naturally fallen, whilst standard LNER types occupied a wide range of numbers.

more leisurely pace of the GN suburban duties, with longer distances between station stops. Similarly, the N7s were more at home on the GE section, where the stations were more closely-spaced and the timetable called for rapid acceleration rather than speed. Thus between 1933 and 1940 eight of the GN-based N7/2s were converted to Westinghouse brake and transferred to the GE section. The remaining eight moved to Bradford in 1942, although they returned south to Hatfield within two years. Meanwhile, most of the N2s drifted back to the GN section.

Modifications

From 1928 onwards the original eleven saturated GER locomotives were fitted with superheaters. This was achieved by building five new boilers and adding superheaters to six of the others. The new boilers had 'pop' safety valves

and most of the existing boilers were similarly fitted. The top feed to the dome was altered to combination injectors and firebox backplate feed, although photographic evidence shows that one or two boilers had conventional side feed to the front of the boiler barrel. From 1926 additional coal rails were added and from 1928 ventilators were added to the cab roofs. However, from 1933 the traditional wooden GE cab roofs were replaced by steel ones to a lower profile (except on the prototype engines 8000 and 8001), with a cutout over the doorway. The two original engines Nos. 8000 and 8001 also gained the larger 8/8½in Westinghouse pumps. Although the LNER had standardised upon the vacuum brake, when building the new 'Quint-Art' articulated carriage sets for the GE suburban lines it had to be conceded that it was impossible to run the GE suburban services with it and thus the new stock was

The final duties of the N7 0-6-2Ts were on the North Woolwich branch, which they continued to work until the end of Great Eastern steam power in September 1962. Here N7/3 No. 69718 departs from North Woolwich with a Palace Gates service formed of a 'Quint-Art' set in January 1960.
(T. Wright 2954)

Notwithstanding the fact that the country was plunged into war, in 1943 a scheme was drawn up to renumber the entire locomotive stock, with certain broad number ranges set aside for locomotives of a particular type. The numbers 1-999 were reserved for the principal express passenger tender locomotives, 1000-1999 for secondary six-coupled passenger and mixed traffic engines, and so on. The N7s fell into the 9000-9999 series reserved for mixed traffic and freight tank engines and they were allocated the numbers 9600-9733.

Having worked out the renumbering scheme in detail, it was nevertheless realised that it would not be practical to implement it until after the war. However, in 1944 two 350hp diesel shunters were built which had been allocated the new numbers 8000 and 8001. Rather than give them temporary numbers, it was instead decided to temporarily renumber the ex-GER N7s 8000-8011 as 7978-7989. The 1943 scheme was finally implemented in 1946, the last N7s being renumbered in January 1947. In the following year the railways were nationalised and the N7s became Nos. 69600-69733.

At the beginning of the war the twelve 'single pipe' N7s Nos. 8000-8011 were at Enfield Town, with the ten 1923-24 engines 7990-7999 at Wood Street on the Chingford branch, supplemented by a number of N7/2s. In 1942 Nos. 8000-8011 were transferred to Wood Street to join them. The remainder of the GE area N7s were distributed between Palace Gates, Hertford East, Ilford, Brentwood, Chelmsford and, of course, Stratford. They covered the whole range of London area suburban services, as well as excursion and holiday traffic, with great success.

The post-war period and nationalisation

Further modifications were made to the brakes of the N7s after the war. The eight remaining vacuum-braked N7/2s at Hatfield were fitted with vacuum-operated push-pull gear in 1949-1951 and these were later joined by three similar conversions from the dual-fitted engines between 1951 and 1957. Meanwhile, the residents living close to Chingford station suddenly developed an aversion to the panting sound of the Westinghouse brake pumps of the N7s and all were fitted with silencers in 1951-1958.

With the introduction of the new Class L1 2-6-4Ts and the inauguration of the Liverpool Street to Shenfield electrification in 1949, many N7s were displaced from suburban work. These engines then moved further afield to country depots, thus displacing the older 2-4-2Ts, which were withdrawn. Others moved away from the GE area to Lincolnshire and Nottinghamshire, among other places. The GN area push-pull conversions worked on the Alexandra Palace branch, or were moved to various GC section branches. The three GE area push-pull engines took up duties on their home section, which by then included the former London, Tilbury & Southend line between Romford and Grays, via Upminster.

Meanwhile, the N7s continued to hold sway on the Enfield and Chingford services from Liverpool Street and by the mid-1950s 40 years of unrelenting toil on these heavy duties were beginning to take their toll. At Enfield and Wood Street depots, the enginemen successfully petitioned the management to re-introduce the time-honoured custom of regular manning of the N7s. Each engine was allocated to two sets of men and both sets then kept their opposite numbers 'on their toes' to ensure that defects were dealt with promptly. There is no doubt that this change of policy enabled the N7s to keep going until finally displaced by electrification of the NE London lines in 1960. At the same time, the crews took more pride in 'their' engines and this resulted in their being kept much cleaner than engines at other depots. The N7s began to acquire unofficial embellishments such as red-painted coupling rods and numberplate backgrounds, or elaborate star designs painted on the smokebox doors.

In 1956, No. 69614 - formerly No. 992E - was selected to act as West Side pilot engine at Liverpool Street. Painted in the lined black BR mixed traffic livery, it was always kept spotless. In the following year No. 69689 was the first of the class to be withdrawn and a further eleven followed in 1958. 40 more followed in 1959, by which time all remaining N7s were on the ex-GE area. The inauguration of the NE London electrification to Enfield, Chingford, Hertford East and Bishops Stortford in 1960 resulted in the scrapping of another 45 N7s, followed by a further 28 the next year. 1962 was the final year of steam power on the GE section south of March and the nine surviving N7s were all Stratford engines. Only one was scrapped prior to the end on 9th September and their main duties were on the Stratford and North Woolwich line, with some trips extended to Palace Gates.

Among the final survivors was No. 69621, the last of the original GE-design engines, and the last locomotive to be built at Stratford Works. It was privately purchased for preservation by Dr. R.F. Youell and was eventually restored to working order at the Stour Valley Railway Preservation Society at Chappel & Wakes Colne (now the East Anglian Railway Museum). It returned to steam in August 1989 at a special event at Southend Victoria to celebrate the centenary of the GER Southend branch and it has since been on loan to several other preserved railways. On 29th March 1991 it was back at Stratford Works to participate in the special event held there to mark the closure of the last-remaining part of the Works. On the same occasion, it was named *A.J. Hill* in honour of the GER Chief Mechanical Engineer responsible for its design and a former Works Manager.

Class N7/2 0-6-2T No. 2650 was one of the 1927 batch built by Beardmore & Co. with steam brakes and vacuum ejectors for the Great Northern line. These engines differed from the N7/1s in having long travel valve gear, higher bunkers with no coal rails, rear pony trucks in place of the radial axle, and other detail differences. The engine is seen here working a stopping passenger train in the late 1930s, following removal of the condensing gear.
(GERS Collection 700.0204)

In the years prior to World War 1 the directors of the Great Eastern Railway were concerned over the poor passenger receipts earned on some of its rural branch lines. It was imperative that operating costs were drastically reduced and an investigation was initiated into the various ways this might be achieved. For some years many of the British main line and, indeed, secondary railways had experimented with - and were in fact operating - steam railcars and auto-trains on lightly-used lines. The GER had lagged behind in the development programme but in 1914 James Holden was given authority to experiment with auto-train working with components almost identical to LBSCR gear. The locomotive was coupled to two converted bogie coaches. The first, GER No. 633, a 48ft 3in clerestory corridor composite coach built in 1904 to Diagram 212, was modified to seat nine first class and thirty third class passengers and was redesignated to Diagram 240. This was placed next to the engine. The second vehicle, clerestory third driving trailer No. 522 originally built in 1906 to Diagram 417 as a corridor lavatory third, after modification had the end compartment converted for the driver and guard and could accommodate 46 third class passengers and was designated to Diagram 433. The two coaches weighed 25 tons 8 cwt and 26 tons 10 cwt respectively.

The auto-train commenced trial running on the Cambridge to Mildenhall branch, where receipts were especially poor, on 5th October 1914, but after several weeks the tests

were transferred to the Somersham to Ramsey High Street branch, where passenger receipts were abysmal. Unfortunately the auto-train was unsuitable for either branch as mixed train working was well established. The train could only operate as a self-contained unit and it was impossible to strengthen the train, so necessary on market days in rural East Anglia, if the engine was propelling. The train was subsequently transferred to the temporarily restored service between White Hart Lane and Cheshunt on the re-opened Churchbury loop line from 1st March 1915. This line was used extensively by munitions workers employed at the Royal Small Arms Factory at Enfield Lock and the Gunpowder Factory at Waltham Abbey and on many occasions the two-coach train was overcrowded. To overcome the problem, a third vehicle, 50ft compartment third No. 524 also to Diagram 417, was converted for auto-train working in 1917 and added to the formation as and when required. No. 524 was identical to sister vehicle No. 522 except that it retained full third class accommodation and because of this difference the vehicle was allocated to Diagram 434. In the meantime to provide cover for Y65 No. 1311, a second locomotive No. 1304 was auto-fitted in November 1915.

After the withdrawal of the service on the Churchbury loop on 1st July 1919, another outlet was found for the auto-train, that of providing an 'off peak' shuttle service on the Palace Gates to Seven Sisters branch in connection with the improved 'Jazz' suburban

service between Liverpool Street and Enfield Town introduced in 1920. The service was inaugurated using Y65 class locomotives Nos. 1304 and 1309, the latter equipped with push-pull gear in May of that year, together with a second two car auto-set comprising GE No. 528, originally built in 1897 to Diagram 209 as 48ft 3in low arc-roofed internal corridor lavatory first/second composite. On conversion this vehicle became a driving composite to Diagram 243. This worked with 50ft elliptical-roofed trailer third GER No. 242, dating from 1913 and built to Diagram 430. Because so few alterations were made, the coach was retained in Diagram 430. Despite Y65 No. 1311 being available as spare engine at Stratford, the availability of just two locomotives at Palace Gates to work these services was always suspect, especially in the event of a failure. Thus in January and February 1921 the position was improved when Y65 Nos. 1303 and 1305 were equipped for push-pull working and sub-shedded at Palace Gates.

No further developments were made until after grouping when the LNER formed a third coaching set in March 1924. This was formed of 48ft 3in low-roofed driving composite GE No. 520, also dating from 1897, and renumbered to LNER 63423 and elliptical-roofed eight compartment trailer third GE No. 273 dating from 1915, renumbered LNER 61488. Once again the driving composite was included in Diagram 243 but the trailer retained its original Diagram 430.

Auto-Trains on the Great Eastern

by Peter Paye

The LNER renumbered the individual vehicles as under:

	GER No.	LNER No.
Set 1		
Driving compartment third	522	61328
Trailer composite	633	63521
Trailer third	524	61330
Set 2		
Driving composite	528	63426
Trailer third	242	61441
Set 3		
Driving compartment	520	63423
Trailer third	273	61488

For normal day-to-day workings only the two-coach sets were employed and Set 1 was retained as spare. If this set was used as maintenance cover the trailer third was not normally used. One set was also spare for maintenance or repair cover whilst the trailer third in Sets 2 and 3 frequently changed over. In the reclassification of locomotive classes introduced by the LNER the Y65 2-4-2Ts were reclassified to F7 and had 7000 added to their GE numbers. In January 1931 F7 No. 8309 was withdrawn from service to be followed by the pioneer GE push-pull locomotive No. 8311 in September of the same year.

By the summer of 1936 the authorities at Norwich were far from satisfied with the performance of the four Clayton steam railcars allocated to the district and plans were prepared to withdraw the vehicles from traffic, once suitable replacements could be found. It was decided the most suitable and cheapest replacement would be push-and-pull trains and authority was duly given to equip four Pollitt ex-Great Central Railway 9G class, LNER F2 class, 2-4-2 tank locomotives with the necessary gear. Accordingly Nos. 5778, 5781, 5783 and 5784 were fitted with vacuum push-and-pull equipment in November 1936 and transferred from their previous haunts around Liverpool and Manchester to the extreme depths of East Anglia, No. 5781 being allocated to Lowestoft and the other three to Norwich.

At the same time Gresley LNER Diagram 63 brake thirds, Nos. 62543 to 62546 inclusive, were converted for push-pull working. They were modified to include large windows at the brake end, a driver's compartment and the necessary operating gear and were reclassified Ordinary Brake Third Driving Carriage, Diagram 254. They were coupled to ex-GER dual-fitted trailer vehicles to form two-coach sets and with the F2s immediately entered service on routes radiating from Lowestoft. Accordingly the four Clayton railcars were withdrawn from traffic in January and February 1937.

In the meantime the three F7s Nos. 8303 and 8305 retained for the Seven Sisters to Palace Gates service were becoming increasingly unpopular with engine crews who considered they were underpowered even for two-coach trains. Taking advantage of a surfeit of ex-North Eastern Railway O class (LNER G5) 0-4-4 tank locomotives displaced by the introduction of steam railcars, the Southern Area authorities readily accepted the offer of more powerful, but older, replacements. Thus in August 1938 G5 No. 2093 was transferred to Stratford and outbased at Palace Gates to supplement the F7s, although initially it was not push-pull fitted. Sister engine No. 441 followed south in November 1938, but was considered unsuitable and returned to the north east in January 1939 to be replaced by sister engine No. 1882. The pair was equipped with compressed air push-pull gear removed from withdrawn F7s in January and February 1939 respectively. Curiously as with the F7 locomotives, the G5s were only fitted with push-and-pull connections at the rear, although electrical connections were fitted at both ends. With the advent of the G5s, F7 No. 8303 was withdrawn from traffic in April 1939.

On 25th May 1939 it was suggested that the passenger train services on the Forncett to

In 1914 the GER fitted Y65 class 2-4-2 tank locomotive No. 1311 with compressed air auto-train equipment and coupled it to two converted bogie coaches for experimental operation on lightly-used branch lines, where operational expenditure exceeded receipts. Here No. 1311 is shown with clerestory composite No. 633 and clerestory third driving trailer No. 522. The auto-train commenced trial running on the Cambridge to Mildenhall line on 5th October 1914 and was later transferred to work the Somersham to Ramsey High Street line, but unfortunately was found unsuitable as mixed train working was well-established on both branches. The train was subsequently transferred to the temporarily restored passenger service between Cheshunt and White Hart Lane on the reopened Churchbury loop line from 1st March 1915.

(GERS collection)

ction

LNER F7 class No. 8309 waiting to depart from Palace Gates with an auto-train for Seven Sisters in June 1930. The shuttle connected at Seven Sisters with the frequent 'Jazz service' operated between Liverpool Street and Enfield Town. No. 8309 was withdrawn from services in January 1931.
(W. Green Collection)

Class Y65 engine No. 8304 was built in 1909 as GER No. 1304 and in November 1915 was the second of the class to be fitted for compressed air-operated auto-train working. It is seen standing in the platform at Seven Sisters station at the head of Auto-Train No. 2 comprising a 50ft third class eight compartment carriage and a 48ft 3in composite driving trailer.

The third class carriage, to diagram 430, was built at Stratford in February 1913 as No. 242 for use on outer suburban trains and was converted for push and pull services in June 1920 but without interior modification. It remained in auto-train use until its withdrawal in February 1957.

The trailer is a former first/third lavatory composite, to diagram 209, built in 1897 for the London and Cromer service. Its alteration to auto-train use entailed the conversion of an end third class compartment for the driver and installation of end windows, becoming diagram 243. The remaining third class compartments were uprated to seconds, as the train worked in the London suburban area, but the alteration was probably confined to new transfers rather than any expenditure on passenger comfort.

Both carriages in the set have recently been repainted – a distinct gloss is visible on the body sides. No. 8304, LNER Class F7, was remumbered by the LNER as No. 7594 and withdrawn in March 1944.
(LPC/John Watling collection)

Wymondham line and the branch line from St. Margarets to Buntingford would be better worked by push-pull trains. It was proposed to equip four trains each consisting of an engine and two coaches, allocating one to the Wymondham line and three to the Hertfordshire branch. The estimated cost was £1,040 but to offset the cost it was proposed to dispense with five guards with an effective saving of £875 per annum. Although the Traffic Committee sanctioned the proposals, nothing came of the scheme. Other schemes were also proposed but failed to reach fruition.

In November 1940 F2 class Nos. 5781 and 5784 were transferred from Lowestoft and Norwich respectivey to Yarmouth South Town and settled to work the Yarmouth to Beccles and Yarmouth to Lowestoft services over the next nine years. Also in 1940 the coaching stock available for push-pull working was augmented when two Diagram 65 coaches, Nos. 3233 and 7572, were converted as OBTDCs and reclassified to Diagram 317. In the following year the remaining F2s at Norwich were transferred to Stratford and outbased at Epping to work the newly-introduced push-pull service to Ongar, inaugurated with the summer timetable. The push-pull trains obviated the necessity to split the formation at Epping, where previously two or three coaches of the train from London were detached and worked forward. The introduction of these trains was unpopular as through coaches were no longer operated between Liverpool Street and Ongar and return. The services of the F2s

in the wilds of Essex was, however, short lived for in 1942 they were transferred to King's Cross to take up duties on the Alexandra Palace push-pull service, which commenced on 7th September of that year. The same year saw more conversions of rolling stock, LNER Diagram 64 vehicle No. 7581 became OBTDC Diagram 320 whilst two Diagram 50 composites, Nos. 32443 and 63265, were also converted for push-pull working.

Push-pull working on the Palace Gates branch was withdrawn as an economy measure in 1942 but Set No. 2, now formed of coaches 61441 and 63423 with F7 No. 8304, was transferred to work the shuttle service between Epping and Ongar from mid-August as replacement for the F2-operated services. However, No. 8304's days were numbered and it was withdrawn from traffic in March 1944, having by then been renumbered in the 1943 scheme to 7594. As a stopgap the G5 locomotives displaced from the Palace Gates line took over the Epping to Ongar services and as two locomotives left little spare capacity in the event of a failure, a third G5 class No. 1780 was transferred to Stratford in May 1944, but was not push-and-pull fitted until February 1945. Nos. 1780, 1882 and 2093 were renumbered 7269, 7279 and 7322 in the LNER 1946 renumbering scheme, but Nos. 7269 and 7279 were sent back to the NE Area from November 1947 to May 1948.

The LNER Southern Area Appendix to the Working Timetable issued in November 1947 showed that push-and-pull trains, restricted to

In July 1951 three G5 class 0-4-4 tank locomotives and two of the two-coach ex-GER push-pull sets were transferred to the Cambridge District to work the Saffron Walden-Audley End-Bartlow branch. No. 67322 is shown near Ashdon pushing a train towards Bartlow in 1956.

(The late Dr. I.C. Allen)

two coaches only, were authorised to run between Epping and Ongar and from Yarmouth South Town to Lowestoft via Gorleston, on the latter route at a maximum speed of 35mph in either direction. Thus with the demise of the

LNER on 31st December 1947, the extant push-pull workings on the GE Section were operated by two Class F2 tanks on the Yarmouth South Town to Lowestoft line and one G5 No. 7322 on the Epping to Ongar shuttle.

In 1949 a pair of class C12 4-4-2 tank locomotives was equipped with vacuum gear to work auto-trains on the shuttle service between Kings Lynn and South Lynn. Here No. 67386 stands at Kings Lynn in May 1957. The C12s were later replaced by N7 class 0-6-2 tank engines.

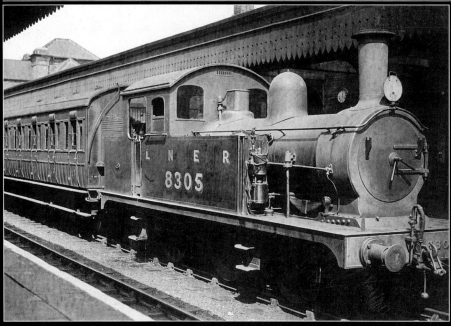

The push-and-pull story was, however, far from finished. British Railways Eastern Region instigated several developments as its officers sought to reduce operating costs. The changes are outside the remit of this article and therefore only a brief summary can be given. Push-pull working was restored on the Seven Sisters to Palace Gates branch in the summer of 1948, using the three Class G5s and the original ex-GE coaching sets. The following year a pair of LNER C12 class, (former GN C2 class) 4-4-2 tank locomotives equipped with vacuum gear commenced working auto-trains between Kings Lynn and South Lynn with LNER stock. Also in 1949 the two F2s in East Anglia were withdrawn and replaced by two ex-GE M15 class, (LNER Class F5) 2-4-2Ts on the Yarmouth to Lowestoft workings. In September of the same year another five F5s were converted for auto-working and were allocated to Epping for the Ongar shuttle. Later another C12 was sent to Yarmouth South Town as maintenance cover for the two F5s.

In July 1951 the three G5 0-4-4Ts and two of the two-coach ex-GER push-pull sets were transferred to the Cambridge District for use on the Audley End-Saffron Walden-Bartlow branch. The introduction of these trains eliminated the time consuming uncoupling, running round and recoupling at either end of the journey on the relatively short route. No mixed trains were worked and a relatively intensive service was operated. Between 1949 and 1954 ten

No.8305 was also built in 1909 as GER No.1304 and equipped for auto-train working in February 1921. It is standing at Palace Gates in charge of Auto-Train No.3. The leading carriage is 50ft third class eight compartment No.61488, built in June 1915 as GER No.273 to diagram 430. It too was withdrawn in February 1957.

The 48ft 3in composite driving trailer is the second of the pair in service at this time. One was GER No.523, LNER No.63426, converted in June 1920 and the other GER No.520, LNER No.63423 converted in March 1924 to replace No.514 of the same type which had been withdrawn following an unspecified mishap. It is not possible to determine which one appears in either view as exchanges took place between the two trains. No.8305 became LNER No.7595 and was withdrawn in April 1943.

(LPC/John Watling collection)

F7 No. 8304 pulling into Noel Park with a Palace Gates to Seven Sisters auto-train on 26th August 1933. All six auto-fitted F7 class engines working on the GE section were fitted with twelve coal rails on the bunker, the remainder of the class having only six, including No. 8307 which was equipped with auto gear and vacuum ejector in December 1924 for working the Aylesbury to Verney Junction line.

(Pamlin Prints)

of Gresley's N class 0-6-2Ts were fitted with vacuum-controlled push-pull gear but did not work any services on the GE section until 1954 when members of the class replaced the F5 locomotives on the Lowestoft to Yarmouth and Lowestoft to Beccles services. In 1955 the solitary auto-train fitted F1 class 2-4-2T spent several weeks on the Epping to Ongar line, covering diagrams after the withdrawal of an F5. The G5s and their antique push-pull stock continued on the Saffron Walden branch until October 1956, when they were replaced by a trio of N7 0-6-2Ts and a pair of Gresley coaching stock sets.

Their arrival was not without their fifteen minutes of fame for a new halt, between Saffron Walden and Ashton to serve Acrow Engineering Works, was opened on 25th March 1957. The first train to call for the opening ceremony was worked by N7 No. 69652 and the driver and fireman were both given a bottle of champagne. Soon after their introduction through trains were introduced between Audley End and Haverhill via Bartlow. In November of the same year the F5s were removed from the Epping to Ongar line after London Transport electrified the route and replaced steam trains with an electric shuttle service. The N7-hauled push-pull trains on the Saffron Walden branch were officially replaced by German-built diesel railbuses from 7th July 1958, but an engine and set of stock was retained in the first week of takeover to cover for failures.

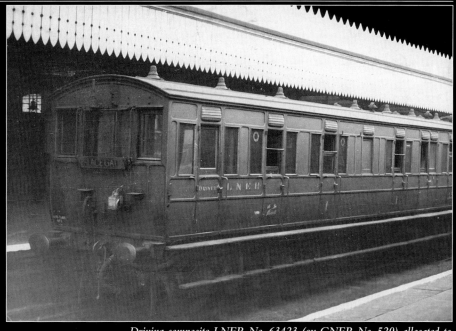

Driving composite LNER No. 63423 (ex-GNER No. 520) allocated to Set No. 3 at Palace Gates. Note the second class compartment behind the driving compartment.
(Photomatic)

The N7s also replaced the C12 4-4-2Ts on the Kings Lynn to South Lynn auto-train service, whilst for a short time one worked the North Walsham to Mundesley and Cromer service in 1954/5. The Kings Lynn to South Lynn shuttle disappeared with the wholesale closure of the former Midland and Great Northern Railway in 1959, whilst the Lowestoft shuttles were an early victim of the advance of diesel multiple units.

Although not strictly within the LNER era, between 1949 and 1954 ten of Gresley's N7 class 0-6-2 tank locomotives were fitted with vacuum-controlled push-pull gear but did not work on any GE section services until 1954 when members of the class replaced F5 class engines on the Lowestoft to Yarmouth and Lowestoft to Beccles services. In 1956 three locomotives and two sets of coaching stock were transferred to Cambridge to work the Saffron Walden branch and here No. 69651 stands at Haverhill after working a through service from Audley End via Bartlow in 1957.
(The late Dr. I.C. Allen)

from THE PLATFORM END
by J.F. Aylard

N2 No.69581 with a CUFFLEY headboard is standing in Platform 6 while waiting for a signal to set off for Wood Green or Bounds Green carriage sidings with empty stock, in November 1957. The headboard indicates that these locos shared their time between two sets of duties. V2 No.60914 is ready to set off in the usual King's Cross clean livery and is probably taking up the 2.00pm duty to Newcastle from Platform 7, a favourite of mine to catch during a lunch-hour. No.60914 looks to be in good nick and this is confirmed by the general repair it had had at Darlington Works barely two months before the shot was taken.

My first recollection of a good vantage point on the LNER was from a lineside path on the west side of Harringay station where I saw a gleaming pale green No. 4476 *Royal Lancer* running light and was hooked on seeing the other 78 members of the class. I soon moved to King's Cross and mingled with the small crowd of grown-up onlookers to be found at the north end of Platform 10 on any day of the week but youngsters in short trousers got pretty short shrift if any questions were asked!

I took one of my first pictures (with the inevitable Box Brownie) in about 1932. It was of No. 2582 *St. Hugo*, leaving with the 10.00am from Platform 10 on a particularly wet day, but I can clearly remember the starting signal on a

short post with the engine standing a few feet beyond it. Another feature at the platform end was the overhead gantry some 20ft high which carried some starting signals plus the main cable-run across the station from the well-known all-electric signal box to the array of points and signals between the mouth of Gasworks Tunnel and the platform ends. The box was built in 1932 in the centre of the station just at the country end of Platforms 5 and 6 and it replaced the two then out-dated East and West manual boxes, the latter being just north of the new box.

This gantry was damaged on 4th February 1945 when A4 No. 2512 stalled in Gasworks Tunnel and, unnoticed by the footplate crew, the train ran back 200 yards into the station

and the last coach was derailed, killing two people and injuring 26. Part of the signal gantry was brought down and unfortunately the breakdown gang took the quick way out by removing damaged sections of the gantry plus otherwise undamaged cables in their haste to clear the site. When the signal engineers found out what had been done, the air around was blue! Chaos reigned as hand signalling had to be used for three weeks until the power system could be restored.

As far as I can remember, it must have been in the autumn of 1947 that, sandwich in hand in my new demob suit during my (official) one hour lunch break from my first job in the City, I first 'made my number' on level terms of age with the group who met at lunchtime. This location was barely 100 yards from Sir Nigel Gresley's one-time office above Platform 10 which is now remembered, some would say rather tardily, by the blue plaque recently placed on the outside of the west-facing station wall below his office window.

LNER assets were all very rundown after six years of prolonged maximum effort while moving wartime traffic of all kinds with a

minimum of maintenance. Locomotives, coaches and stations were in a generally unkempt and grubby condition which did not make for the attractive photographs of 1939 even if sufficient film had been available, which was not the case.

The permanent way on the Great Northern section was very rundown and maintenance gangs were short-staffed, so consequently all lines were subject to a maximum speed limit of 60mph. The necessity of this limit was shown by the weak spots which were soon to manifest themselves only too clearly at Hatfield, Marshmoor and New Southgate all in the year after I joined the group. Very fortunately there was only one casualty (Driver Bill Hoole's fireman in the New Southgate accident) but the position would have been much worse if the rolling stock in each case had not been held upright and prevented from over-riding by Gresley's far-seeing use of buckeye couplings.

As to the subjects discussed by the group, top of the list was the great enigma concerning what Doncaster Works was going to build when it completed the last two A2/3 Pacifics to Thompson's design in August and September

TOP: *B1 No.61299 of 38C Leicester shed, a very unusual loco at King's Cross, is about to leave (when they get round to shutting the doors) on 6th September 1957. But judging by the staff member who is standing with his hands behind his back, this is not imminent. The train is hard to identify as it clearly is not the 2.00pm for Edinburgh which could be expected to leave from Platform 10 at the time on the clock. It is also unusual in that it is made up of only seven or eight coaches at a time when most ECML trains were formed of ten or twelve vehicles, and hence it is standing well within the main building. After the lapse of 44 years I can only recall that it was a special of some kind but even that is hard to identify, as where would punters pay to go to while leaving King's Cross on a Friday at, say, 2.10pm? Not football? Anyway, the shot shows (a) the window forming western half of the station front, clean for a change, (b) the mass of luggage and parcels which lay handy to stow (pinch?) in some luggage van which would be nominated to stop at the loading point, (c) over the cab roof of the loco the top of the luggage lift which gave access to the basement.*

LOWER: *This scene shows the western edge of King's Cross station. Platforms 14/15 of the suburban station can be seen on the left where trains for Hatfield, Hertford North and Welwyn Garden City started their journey. On 2nd July 1955 N2 No.69498 is standing in Platform 15 ready to take an empty set of five new BR non-corridor bogie stock to Western sidings at Finsbury Park and Bounds Green. Platform 16 is on the right at a slightly lower level where the track has just climbed at a gradient of 1 in 48 in the Hotel Curve Tunnel over a curve of eight chains radius from the Widened Lines which run from Moorgate and South London. This train is headed by N2 No.69532. If I have read the headboard correctly, it is going to Welwyn Garden City and is hauling two Quad-art sets forming eight articulated cars. Above the first coach of this train can be seen the awning to Platform 16 and above the cab of N2 can be seen the awning to Platform 17 which ceased to be used after World War II. Further to the right can be seen a third N2 which is standing to await its next turn of duty and is in the milk dock which used to receive GN milk traffic.*

TOP: *A4 No.60015* Quicksilver *was one of the engines specially nominated in 1959 by King's Cross shed for use on the 9.30am 'Elizabethan' which ran non-stop to Edinburgh in 7hours 35mins. This meant that the engine would go into Doncaster Works in May so that it was ready to take part in the, generally, thirteen weeks' running in June-September. The Shed Master, Mr. P. Townend, took a close personal interest in the running and details concerning the amount of oil used in lubricating the main bearings had to be reported to him at the end of play for the day. In this way he kept under review the need for any attention to be given to the main bearings should consumption increase, and avoid delays in traffic. The picture was taken on 15th June 1959, the first day of the service and he can be seen on the right of the cab window as the loco backs down on to its train which had also been given special attention to achieve East Coast standards. I should point out that he clearly isn't dressed appropriately for a trip to Edinburgh!*

LOWER: *As No.60108* Gay Crusader *is leaving Platform 10 on 31st July 1952 on the 'White Rose' 9.18am to Leeds. A local train which has just left the suburban station hauled by N2 No.69556 is seen ahead of the Pacific and an A2 acting as standing pilot in the station loco can be seen just ahead of the N2. The N2 and A3 will climb the 1 in 105 bank inside the joint bores of Gasworks Tunnel side by side until the A3 overtakes the N2. The noise and smoke forced into the compartments of the local train through the closed windows at every stroke of the A3s cylinders just a few feet away in the semi-dark with only a weak gas lamp is an experience which is not easily forgotten!*

1947, Nos. 523 *Sun Castle* and 524 *Herringbone*, not perhaps everyone's obvious choice for a favourite Pacific name! The next batch of locomotives was to be designed by A.H. Peppercorn (who had succeeded Thompson) and drawings and photographs would be published in December when it was rumoured that he would revert to many of the much-loved Gresley features which Thompson had not favoured.

In the event, the Platform 10 group-members' prayers were largely answered and a combined sigh of relief was clearly audible when the first pictures of A2 No. 525, named after the great man himself, appeared. The list of names to be used was a point of some general interest as were the sheds to which they were to be allocated. I remember making great efforts to enter the holy of holies, Top Shed, as it was known at King's Cross, to photograph the magnificent beast.

Other new features which were worthy of mention at that time included the almost-universal use that was made of new B1s by the shed master at King's Cross. He had nine allocated and on a busy Saturday in August 1947, thirteen of the class were noted, the second most numerous type to be seen. B1 No. 1200 of King's Cross was sent to Newcastle on the 1.07pm with twelve bogies and took 30 minutes to pass Potters Bar, twelve miles away but admittedly much of it climbing continuously for eight miles at 1 in 200. No. 1114 followed on the 3.40pm to Leeds with eleven on. Even a B1 was not unknown on the down *Aberdonian* with its batch of heavy sleepers plus the inevitable diner on the rear to be detached at York.

The forthcoming nationalisation of the railways on 1st January 1948 was frequently discussed and efforts were made to assess what form the livery for passenger locomotives would take. After all, the *Railway Magazine* had shown a B1 painted in Post Office red in the frontispiece to the magazine as one possibility! The LNER published plans to build 25 diesel-electric locomotives to work on the East Coast Main Line with two 1,600hp units per train, replacing 32 Pacifics. This brought cold shivers down the spine of members of the group. All was not black, however, as a series of inter-Regional locomotive trials was announced early in 1948 and the timings of the workings of the 'opposition' locomotives on the then Eastern Region and visiting King's Cross were eagerly sought.

The founder member and pivot of the Platform 10 group for many years up to the end of steam in June 1963 was undoubtedly Eric Neve, simply because he was by far the most knowledgeable non-railwayman around. What he didn't see or know about wasn't worth recording. He thus became the central source of information at a time when unlike today, there were only two or three monthly magazines to spread the gospel. He was able to move through closed platform end barriers which could be opened without the intervention of a member of the staff, by pressing one's foot on a treadle just by the gate post! If you were really thin, it was known for someone to squeeze between the two halves of the gate while they technically remained shut!

It may not be generally known that Eric was a thoroughbred GNR man as his father had been a signalman who started work at Peakirk station, the first on the Lincoln line from Peterborough, where he had met his

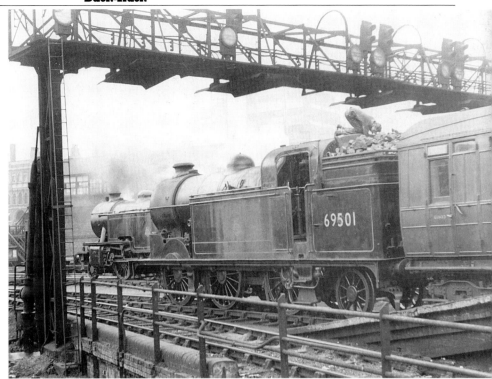

wife. He moved to Cemetery box near New Southgate (where Eric lived for many years) and then to King's Cross station, a most highly-rated post as it was quite unlike any lineside box. The staff frequently had to originate several trains simultaneously, pair locomotives with the right stock in the right platform and get them away to time, a juggling act that required a cool head and allowed no room for mistakes. All this work had to be performed in the small space between the mouth of Gasworks Tunnel and the platform ends, with the record for the shortest turnround time for stock arriving and departing in steam days being an unbelievable nine minutes. Could that be achieved in 1999, I wonder?

By virtue of his close knowledge of the workings of the station (much, no doubt, learnt in his youth when his father was a power in the land by virtue of his important job), the staff saw him everyday over many years and thought he was a member of the station security team.

Eric kept a sharp observation on train movements from his house and his notes from the mid-1920s onward make absorbing reading as he saw such rarities as A3 No. 2748 *Colorado* when working from King's Cross in March 1929 before it began an 18½ year-long stint at Carlisle Canal shed after which it was next to unknown in London. D49 No. 245 *Lincolnshire* together with the P2s Nos. 2001 and 2002 all on trials plus the early silver A4s and the return to traffic of GNR single No. 1 are also to be found in the notes.

Other friends I can remember include Leslie Burley, who had an encyclopaedic knowledge of railway working and especially the footplate crews and their steeds. It was he who collected data from a small team (which included someone who compiled the duty rosters in Top Shed) so that he could tabulate the priceless details of every A4 working on the three streamlined trains on every day over the four years that they ran. (This has been reprinted in the *Gresley Observer*).

Leslie recalls that the meetings were under way by October 1945. Derrick Dant, the well-known photographer, was a regular attender. He was always keen to recount his latest efforts to spur the ER management to ensure the timely departure of the 5.58pm King's Cross to Welwyn Garden City which ran non-stop to Potters Bar (his home station), otherwise known as the 'Potters Bar Barbarian'. His chief adversary at the time was Inspector Ilsley and neither was known to pull his punches. When the special train which was hauled to Doncaster by the last Ivatt large Atlantic on its final run before withdrawal had a hot box on one of the two GC dining cars when returning to London, it was this inspector who knew where to find the key to the closed signal box so that the car could be detached at Biggleswade - under the doormat!

Peter Coster, now chairman of the Gresley Society, is another name that immediately comes to mind as someone who can recall in great detail the engine workings and rosters of the Top Link footplate crews whom he knew very well. Brian Perren, now a well-known writer and author on British and French railways, was a very regular member. Reg Lucas, whose forte was to keep accurate records of station track layouts and details of signalling arrangements, and David Tellwright, a BR staff member and valued contact who could be relied on to produce coaching stock details from internal records,

TOP: *A non-condensing N2 No.69501 is standing in Platform 15 and the fireman has an important problem with something in the bunker for which he is prepared to risk injuring himself. Note the firing shovel which has been jammed behind the hand rail to give him a grip to lower himself back to civilisation! The loco is likely to be about to more a Quad-art set of eight cars out to the sidings. I doubt very much if No.69501 would be used for passenger purposes as the crews at King's Cross and Hornsey were loath to use a non-condensing engine other than on light duties. The L1 behind it would be on the 5.58pm first stop at Potters Bar (generally known by the No.10 'Mafia' as 'The Barbarian') and then all station to Welwyn Garden City. Much hung on the punctuality of this train and a member of the 'Mafia' made it his personal responsibility to see that justice   prevailed. He was always in close touch with Running Inspector Ilsley who represented the Eastern Region in any questions concerning the timekeeping of this train. The rest of us just stood back and watched the sparks fly when 5.59pm arrived and the train was still in the platform!*

LOWER: *A3 No.60102 Sir Frederick Banbury is shown leaving Platform 8 at 9.00am in November 1957 as the first part of the 'White Rose' for Leeds, while A1 Bois Roussel carrying the train headboard is standing in Platform 10 to form the main train leaving at 9.20am. At the extreme right the train guard can be seen making his way to the rear of the train. He is carrying his company issue rectangular bag no doubt containing his lunch, flags, log book, special train notices and book of rules plus a paper to tell him the runners for the day! In addition he has what looks like an old gas-mask case, a suitcase in his right hand and his lamp!*

TOP: *LMR Class 5 No.44911 is seen standing in Platform 4 on an up outer suburban train possibly from Cambridge on 7th May 1956. This loco had been transferred from Chester to the King's Cross area so that tests could be carried out on this class to see how it worked when the new ATC was in use. Alongside is A2 No.60500* Edward Thompson *in Platform 5.*

LOWER: *B1 No.61142 is passing King's Cross Signal Box on 17th June 1957 as it backs into Platform 6 to pick up the stock for an afternoon train, the 4.05pm to Cleethorpes. Having been allocated to Immingham depot very soon after it was built in April 1947, it had been seen regularly on London trains during the previous ten years. The fact that it is reversing is confirmed by the position of the valve gear. The Box played a very important part in the day-to-day working of the southern end of the ECML. It was in phone connection with all the larger boxes which carried out regulatory functions in maintaining good timekeeping throughout the network. This phone link, plus that of the usual box-to-box bell codes and also a morse code audio link broadcast to wayside boxes, was always visible from the track and could be recognised as a mass of wires which were carried on numerous rows of insulators. Heaven defend any driver who was shunting in the vicinity of such telegraph poles near marshalling yards or wayside sidings and damaged, let alone demolished, one of the poles, as vengeance would strike with great effect as the system was brought to a halt until signal fitters could be summoned to make repairs.*

The men in the box had the responsibility of ensuring first the stock and then the loco were united in the right platform and to time. The road had to be cleared for the departures despite all the light engine and empty stock movements to say nothing of all the other trains themselves, including sometimes Royal Trains.

kept us company. There were also Tony Scarsbrook, a keen photographer, and finally Frank Giles whom I knew when we both stood guard at the brick sidings by Wood Green Tunnel Box after school in the late 1930s and who has an amazing facility for knowing where to find obscure facts from the wealth of railway literature, particularly in the *Railway Magazine* and the works of Dr. Tuplin.

Others whom I knew only by name but who were all residents of Barnet (the home of many railwaymen including Oliver Bulleid and Driver Sparshatt to name only two who lived barely a ¼ mile apart at either end of the road where this was written) were Messrs. Ball (who worked at the Railway Clearing House), Stevens (an early member of the Stephenson Locomotive Society and a photographer whose work appeared in the *Railway Magazine* in the inter-war years) and John Phillips, who was a friend of Leslie Burley. These aficionados came from all walks of life, civil servants, bank, railway, oil and steel industry managers, an official from the High Court in the Strand, but strangely no members of the Cloth who generally seem to appear in any group of railway enthusiasts.

The names of the No. 1 (top) link drivers of that era were known to everyone in the group and they could be recognised from the lineside even when partially obscured in the cab. The roll in the mid-1950s (and their regular A4s) read as follows:- Ted Clowes (13), Bert Cull (28), Fred Dines (28), Jim 'Economy' Edwards (33), Arthur Ferrington (14), Shirley Frost, George Graham (17), Green, Alf Guymer (13), Ted Hailstone (14), Percy Heaven (25), Bill Hoole (7), 'Peanut Joe' or 'Jonah' Howard (22), Arthur Marrable, famous for his part at the regulator in the official film of the 'Elizabethan' (17), Alf Smith (22), Charlie Simmons (7), Sid Tappin (13), Tee, Warley and Harry Willers (10). Incidentally, Charlie Simmons, like many railwaymen, was active in local government and was three times Mayor of Finsbury. Joe Howard took B1 No. 61251 *Oliver Bury* on the 1948 inter-Region locomotive exchanges and got some magnificent work out of her (or him!) which was arguably better than anyone did afterwards. He beat the Stanier Class 5 and the 'Modified Hall'. This fact became rather overlooked as the 'West Country' wiped the floor with the 4-6-0s in all respects (particularly on the Highland line) except in those areas that really matter - coal and water consumption.

Another name from the Top Link at around this date which must be included is that of Horace Duckmanton. He was held in great esteem both by the platform-enders and, more important, by the Management. He was a real professional, always punctual, highly reliable, and a real engineman to his fingertips. It was he who ran No. 60156 for 96,000 miles in a year with no failures AND he had a clean record on retirement. You can't do better than that.

I would like to thank all the people who have generously written to me about the old days, thus supplying much that is written here, and in particular Peter Coster who even at this late date was able to recall for me so graphically many of the details I have quoted concerning the Top Link men of the 1950s. One thing that has become clear to me when writing this note is how much we all owe to the founder and anchorman of the group, the late Eric Neve who had a marvellous rapport with railway staff and was kind enough to pass on his nuggets of information so obtained to our group.

TSS Arnhem *was the last vessel constructed for the LNER, making her maiden voyage on 26th May 1947. She was built by John Brown (Clydebank) Ltd. Her last sailing was on 27th April 1968 after which she was sold to T.W. Ward at Inverkeithing for breaking up in August 1968. This view was taken at Parkeston Quay in July 1966.*

TSS Avalon *at Parkeston Quay on 28th June 1964. Built by Alexander Stephen & Sons Ltd. of Linthouse, on the Clyde, she took up duty on the Harwich station in July 1963. She made her last sailing to Hoek van Holland in December 1974 and was converted to a roll on/roll off ferry for the Fishguard—Rosslare route and later the Holyhead—Dun Laoghaire run in 1975.* Avalon *was sold for scrap to Pakistan in 1981.* (G.J. Child)

SAILING
from HARWICH

Photographs by JOHN EDGINGTON

A service was started by the Great Eastern Railway from Harwich Town to Rotterdam in 1863. In 1863 the English terminal was altered to a completely new site two miles west of Harwich called Parkeston Quay, named after the chairman of the GER. The Netherlands terminal was transferred to Hoek van Holland at the western end of the 'New Waterway' in 1893. A service is still maintained by Stena Line's high-speed craft. The Harwich—Zeebrugge train ferry was inaugurated on 24th April 1924 with three train ferries which had been built for the Richborough—Dunkerque service in the 1914-18 war. Great Eastern Train Ferries Ltd. was taken over by the LNER in 1934. The service was suspended in 1939 but was resumed in 1946 with the one vessel which had survived the war. Final closure of the service occurred on 31st January 1987.

This feature takes a look at the last of the LNER's ships on the Harwich sailings together with their British Railways successors.

....SAILING FROM HARWICH

TSMV St. George, *off Parkeston Quay in September 1969, was the first roll on/roll off ship for the Harwich—Hoek van Holland service and was built by Swan Hunter (Shipbuilders) Ltd. at Walker-on-Tyne, making her first voyage on 17th July 1968. Here last sailing was on 5th June 1983 and she was sold to Greece in 1984.*

TSMV Cambridge Ferry *was built by Hawthorn Leslie (Shipbuilders) Ltd. of Hebburn-on-Tyne and made her maiden voyage on 2nd January 1964. In 1977 the boat deck was extended to carry 25 more trade cars (as shown in this picture, taken in the River Stour off Harwich in July 1983). After the closure of the Zeebrugge service,* Cambridge Ferry *was used on freight services from Dover, Fishguard and Stranraer, being withdrawn after her last sailing from Stranraer on 16th March 1992. She was sold to Italian buyers on 21st April 1992.*

TOP: *TSMV* Essex Ferry, *off Harwich in September 1969, was built by John Brown & Co. (Clydebank) Ltd. and made her first sailing on 15th January 1957. Later, in 1957, the stern was modified to fit the Dunkerque linkspan. The vessel was sold to Medway Secondary Metals Ltd. of Rainham, Kent, in April 1983 and was converted to a pontoon to assist in raising a capsized oil rig* Alexander Kielland.

BELOW: *TSMV* Norfolk Ferry *was also from John Brown & Co. (Clydebank) Ltd. and made her maiden voyage in July 1951. She inaugurated the Harwich—Dunkerque service on 2nd October 1967 and is pictured here at the Harwich train ferry berth. The ship was placed in reserve in 1980 and was sold in April 1983 for breaking up at Vlissingen.*

LNER
survivors

O f the 'Big Four' companies, the locomotives of the LNER fared least well in the preservation era. As fate would have it, its locomotives after withdrawal were mostly cut up fairly swiftly and only one – a B1 4-6-0 – is believed to have reached the 'locomotive graveyard' of Woodham's scrapyard at Barry, South Wales, from which so much of the preserved locomotive fleet was rescued. Consequently, there are fewer LNER locomotives still to be seen than there are of the other three pre-1948 companies, but we have reason to be for ever grateful to some of the preservation pioneers for the famous names which are still with us. Here are three of the best-known.

To start, here is probably the most famous locomotive of them all – A3 Pacific No.4472 Flying Scotsman. Its credits are legion: the British Empire Exhibition in 1924, the first London–Edinburgh 'non-stop' in 1928, the first official 100mph in 1934. On its withdrawal from service in 1963 it was bought by Alan Pegler and became one of the first privately-owned locomotives to haul special trains over BR tracks. Its subsequent colourful history encompasses visits to the USA and Australia as well as two more changes of ownership, but fortunately No.4472 is still with us – and still steaming! Here it is during the first phase of its preservation career well away from home territory as it arrives at Basingstoke with a Pullman special to Farnborough on 12th September 1964. (Derek Penney)

One of the LNER's most eyecatching and distinctive designs was the A4 streamlined Pacific, introduced in 1935. Their unmistakeable outline and striking liveries – silver grey at first, then garter blue with red wheels – summed up LNER style and they were, of course, outstanding performers; the world speed record holder Mallard is amongst their number. Six of the class are preserved, including one in the USA and one in Canada. The four British-based survivors – including Mallard in the National Collection – have all worked in preservation but the most active, very appropriately, has been No.4498 Sir Nigel Gresley. The A4 Locomotive Society saved the locomotive in 1966 and it became one of the early main line pioneers in 1967. In preservation No.4498 has always run without the lower skirting over the wheels but has always presented a fine sight, as here at Appleby with a southbound Settle-Carlisle line special on 27th October 1984. (Alan Tyson collection)

Notwithstanding the deserved reputation of the Pacifics, many would claim the LNER's and Gresley's most successful design to be the V2 2-6-2. Primarily built for heavy fast freights, the V2s soon showed their paces on passenger trains and were perfectly capable of standing in for Pacifics on the top expresses. During the Second World War the class was responsible for prodigious feats of haulage and continued to play an important part in East Coast Main Line traffic into the 1960s. Only one of the class has survived, the pioneer No.4771 Green Arrow in the National Collection. A main line performer from the 1970s to the present day, Green Arrow's travels have taken it to unfamiliar locations such as Holyhead with the 'North Wales Coast Express' in August 1991. (D.W. Mosley)

Atlantic